My Story

Inside and Out

Robert Gogerly

BookLocker
Saint Petersburg, Florida

Published by BookLocker.com, Inc., St. Petersburg, Florida.

Printed on acid-free paper.

BookLocker.com, Inc.
2020

First Edition

For my loving mother Maud, my effervescent daughter Rachel and my dear brother Richard.

Acknowledgements

My thanks go out to the many people who encouraged and supported me in this project. To my boyhood friend Dr.Quintus deZylva who urged me to do this for years. Also from those days back in Kandy, Sri Lanka, Lisa Enqvist, who encouraged me and provided me with the links I needed to further my efforts. To Jeanette Gallant and Preethi Mendis who shared the progress of my manuscript and helped and supported me with comments to keep me on track. To Judith Talanoa who helped with editing and proof-reading.

Thanks also to Angela Hoy CEO of BookLocker who took me on as a first-time author, Ali Esther for formatting the manuscript to make it ready for publication and helping me fix my 'typos' and to Todd Engel for designing the cover.

And last, but by no means least, my wife Jan, who helped immeasurably bringing me cookies and cups of tea while I worked, whose help with the title and 'eagle eye' proof-reading kept me on the straight and narrow. Again, my heartfelt thanks to you all.

My Sri Lanka

Prologue

Bathed in the waves of the vast Indian Ocean, nestled at the southern tip of the land that is home to a fifth of the world's population (India), lies a relatively tiny island paradise. Fanned by warm tropical breezes and washed by cleansing tropical rain, it is home to gentle people friendly and uncomplicated, magnanimous and welcoming, with a generosity of spirit that is unique in this day and age.

It wasn't always like this.

When you read the history of this land that follows, you may wonder if I have made a mistake in my description, but I am talking of the people at the heart of Sri Lanka, the Sinhalese to whom the island truly belongs. These people have had to endure invasions by foreign powers through centuries, resulting in conflicts of culture, religion, and politics. Throughout all this, their inherent nature has simmered and survived and the island is blessed with their presence, just as they are blessed with its richness in culture and natural resources of which they are an integral part.

The island has been known by various names throughout its chequered history. The Arabs and Persians knew it as Serendib, the Portuguese called it Ceilao, the Dutch, Zeilan, and the British, Ceylon. It remained thus until in 1972 when in a new Constitution it was named Sri Lanka which means 'Resplendent Land.'

The background to my story is a brief history of Sri Lanka whose original inhabitants date back some three thousand years.

Sri Lanka is a tiny tear-shaped island at the southern tip of India. Its area is 65,610 kilometres. The distance from north to south is 445 kilometres and east to west is 225 kilometres, with a coastline of 1340 kilometres. It is about the size of Tasmania or less than 30 percent the size of the state of Victoria, in Australia. It is half the size of England and about the same size as West Virginia in the U.S.A. It has a central mountainous terrain and low lying plains stretching around them to the sea. The tallest mountain in Sri Lanka is Pidurutalagala at 2524 metres (8281 feet) in elevation. It is only 172 kilometres from the Capital Colombo on the west coast but takes 5 hours to traverse over winding mountainous roads. It is 8 degrees north of the equator. Its population in 2020 is 21.4 million but under 8 million at the start of this story in 1938.

Sri Lanka's original inhabitants were the Veddahs (called Yakshas) and were the first indigenous islanders. They were hunter – gatherers. About 500 BC the Sinhalese arrived led by Vijaya. Buddhism was introduced in 260 BC by Mahinda and it soon became a part of Sinhalese culture.

When the Portuguese arrived in 1505 there were three main kingdoms, the Kingdom of Jaffna in the north, the Sinhalese Kingdom of Kandy in the central hills, and the Kingdom of Kotte near Colombo on the west coast. The Portuguese conquered Jaffna and the low-lying west coast and then the east. There was resistance to Christianity which they introduced to the island. Buddhists fled to Kandy in the hill country which became the centre of the Buddhist faith.

The Dutch arrived in 1602. In exchange for Sri Lankan autonomy, the Kandyan King Rajasinghe 11 gave the Dutch monopoly on the spice trade. They ruled the country for a hundred and forty years and were more enterprising than the Portuguese. Canals were built to transport cinnamon and other crops. The canals around Negombo are a legacy of their reign.

The British gained control when the Dutch ceded Sri Lanka to them in 1796. They made the island a colony in 1802, finally annexing Kandy in 1815. Kandy had retained its sovereignty for 339 years from 1476 before King Sri Vikrama Rajasinghe was captured by the British on 15 February 1815, betrayed by some of his ministers who actively conspired against him by providing intelligence to the British.

With the capture of King Sri Vikrama Rajasinghe Kandy was the last bastion to fall to foreigners, which meant the whole Island was now annexed by the British. King Sri Vikrama Rajasinghe was the last ruling monarch of the island. He built the Dalada Maligawa, the temple which still houses Buddha's Tooth Relic. He also built the scenic Kandy Lake, still a tourist attraction.

By the 1830s British settlers had begun to arrive. Coffee was a major crop in Sri Lanka at the time and a blight, known as coffee leaf rust, destroyed the entire crop. Coffee and rubber were replaced by the famous Ceylon tea. Tea plantations spread widely across the hill country, whole hills being covered by tea bushes. Tamil labourers were imported from South India to work on the tea plantations.

There was a new Constitution introduced in 1931 which granted universal suffrage. To put things in context, seventy - five percent of the population were Sinhalese, eleven percent Sri Lankan Tamil, nine percent Moor and four percent Indian Tamil. The population of the island was just under eight million.

In the late 1930's Hitler was running rampant in Europe. The Second World War was declared on 1 September 1939 ending on 2 September 1945. Sri Lanka was a British base, its strategic position just south of India making it Britain's gateway to the Far East, and a critical location in its war effort. It was also shared as an American military base.

PART ONE

Footprints

Chapter One

This is the background of my story which begins in 1938.

In Europe, Hitler's plans for expansion commenced with the occupation of Austria in March. It became apparent that Poland would be his next target and Britain and Poland entered into a military alliance. The British, though still hopeful of a peaceful solution to Hitler's designs on Poland, were preparing for war.

In Ceylon life moved at a leisurely pace. In a quiet seaside suburb just north of the capital Colombo, I came screaming into the world on 12 May 1938, eldest son of Robert and Maud Gogerly. Robert was a descendant of Rev. Daniel John Gogerly, a Methodist missionary who arrived in Ceylon from London in 1818.

He was the first person to start a Buddhist – Christian dialogue, and, as a keen student of Pali, he went on to produce the first Pali dictionary. He studied Buddhism and could preach in three different languages – English, Sinhalese, and Pali (an ancient Indian language aligned to Buddhism).

My mother Maud (nee Hepponstall) was a descendant of William Hepponstall who arrived in Ceylon from West Riding in Yorkshire, England in the early nineteenth century to become a Tea Planter.

Over the generations, after they arrived in Ceylon, the Gogerly's were assimilated into the Ceylonese way of life and culture and I consider myself privileged to have grown up in an environment that fostered compassion, tolerance, and generosity of spirit. The Gogerly families were invariably large, (as most were in those times) and some inter-marriages between them and Sinhalese girls cemented this assimilation.

My dad was lean, handsome, and just over six feet in height, with attractive green eyes which held a mischievous gleam, or so I'm told.

My mum was pretty, had dark hair, bright brown eyes, and a petite figure.

Dad worked as Sales Manager at Millers Limited, a Department Store specializing in the distribution of various brands of dry food for brand names like Bonlac, Kraft, Nestle, and Cadbury. They were also distributers of photographic equipment for Kodak and printing equipment.

We moved to a seaside suburb of Colombo just across from the beach with my grandparents (Dad's parents Joe and Ethel) living in a large house within walking distance in Quarry Road. We were constant visitors.

Hitler's rampage in Europe expanded in 1938-39 with the annexure of Czechoslovakia and Austria. On September 1, 1939, Nazi German forces invaded

Poland. England and France declared war on Germany. Japan and China were at war and Ceylon had become the meat in the sandwich. Hostilities had not reached Ceylon yet but the tension of a world at war pervaded the island when Britain used Ceylon as a British base in its strategic position as a gateway to the Far East. They were to be joined later by American forces.

My sister Barbara was born on 26 September 1940, my brother Alex a year later on 16 September 1941.

In December Japan entered the war against the USA with an attack on Pearl Harbour in Hawaii.

Hong Kong was taken in December and Singapore fell in February 1942. Britain strengthened its military presence on the island. With America joining Britain and its allies, battlefronts were hotting up across the globe.

On 4th April 1942 Canadian Squadron Leader Leonard Birchall on a reconnaissance mission from Colombo spotted a fleet of ships heading towards Ceylon and reported its position to his base in Colombo. His plane was shot down by the Japanese and he was taken captive.

The next morning, Easter Sunday 5 April 1942, Nagumo launched an air raid against Ceylon. Irrespective of Birchall's warning, the unexpected airstrike was a complete surprise. The British radar was down for maintenance. The first attack wave of Japanese planes took off just before sunrise, led by Captain Matsuo Fushido, who led the Pearl Harbour attack. Churches were packed for Easter services and when the attack commenced people scrambled for air raid shelters. The air battle lasted for nearly half an hour. The Allied Forces were able to shoot down some of the enemy aircraft near St. Thomas' College and on Galle Face Green. A bomb fell on a Mental Hospital which was mistaken for Army Barracks. There were severe casualties on both sides but the Japanese were surprised by the ferocious retaliation they encountered and recognised that they lacked the resources for a major operation against Ceylon.

British Prime Minister, Winston Churchill, considered this the most dangerous moment of the Second World War, and the one which caused him the greatest alarm was when the news was received that the Japanese Fleet was heading for Ceylon. Squadron Leader Leonard Birchall was regarded as the "Saviour of Ceylon."

I was just under four years old on this Easter Sunday and all I can remember is the frightening sounds of the air raid sirens as we scrambled to the air-raid shelter at the back of my grandparent's house.

On 2 December 1942, my second brother Richard was born.

The British Army was recruiting at this time and my Dad enlisted in the R.A.S.C (Royal Army Service Corps) in Colombo and was part of the Middle East

Forces (M.E.F.) I remember his first day in the Army. He came home with his hair cut short in a khaki soldier's uniform and I looked at him kind of surprised because he looked so different. Then he was in the Army barracks and we only saw him when he was allowed leave to come home.

Then came that day in May 1943.

We were at my Aunt's place in Kandy some 116 kilometres (72 miles) from Colombo in the central hill country. It was a house on Peradeniya Road and still looks the same today (2020) as it did back then. The mood was sombre and a feeling of uncertainty was in the air. We were all gathered at the front porch and Mum was crying. Dad was in his army uniform and had his bags packed. A rickshaw pulled up on the road outside the house, drawn by a lanky 'rickshaw' man.

A rickshaw was a two-seater carriage with large wheels, an open pull-up canopy behind the seat and a yolk between which the man pulling the rickshaw positioned himself. This was an accepted mode of transport of the times and they were the first 'taxis'.

Dad hugged and kissed us all and gave Mum a big hug and a goodbye kiss and boarded the rickshaw with his bags. The rickshaw man pulled up the yolk to waist height and flip-flopped his way down the road in his leather sandals.

We watched him till we couldn't see him anymore and went back inside the house. Mum was crying and we felt a sense of apprehension. A little later we all gathered in the yard at the back of the house from where we could see the railway track. We knew Dad had gone to the Kandy Railway station and we waited to see the 3 o'clock train to Colombo on its way. About 3.10 we heard the steam train come chugging down the line tooting its way down the track, grey smoke billowing from the engine funnel. It was packed with khaki-clad soldiers bulging out of the doors and windows, waving to relatives and friends watching it go by. We didn't see Dad in the mass of soldiers but we waved anyway.

Then he was gone.

He had joined the Middle East Forces and was to be stationed at Egypt in the heart of the action in a World War that was devastating humanity.

We didn't know when, or if, we'd see him again and Mum was sobbing uncontrollably. We weren't fully aware of all that was happening, our ages ranging from five months (Richard) to just under five years (me). We had no idea what the future held and came back inside after the train disappeared out of sight, to pick up the pieces of uncertainty with a distinct sense of foreboding.

But life has to go on and time went by. There was poor Mum left with four children to take care of by herself, not knowing what the future held for anyone. But family ties were strong and my aunts and uncles came to the fore to help Mum cope. My Uncle Ric (Mum's brother) the doctor in the family, took on the responsibility of my upkeep. Mum's sisters, Aunt

Gwen, and Aunt Gladys said they would help with looking after Barbara, Alex, and Richard.

At that time we all stayed at that large house in Kandy with Aunt Gwen and Uncle Willie. They had two teenage daughters, Dorothy and Moira. Their son Francis was just about to head off to medical school. It was a full house and we were lucky that it had six bedrooms. My memories of that time included seeing American army trucks parked outside and American soldiers forming friendships with the family and no doubt flirting with Dorothy and Moira, who were in their late teens.

Then it was time for me to go to school.

Chapter Two

My time at Kingswood College commenced in October 1943 in Primary School Kindergarten. I remember the day Mum enrolled me and I walked into the play area outside what was to be my first classroom. There was a climbing frame in the quadrangle with four square-shaped outside sections, with wooden rungs and a central section that extended up about eighteen inches higher than the outer sections. A few boys were on the frame and a boy named Derrick was atop the central section.

When he saw me approach he said, "Hi! I'm Derrick. You're new, aren't you? Come on up and play." That made me feel comfortable and I formed a friendship with Derrick that lasted all through my school years into adulthood. We were good friends until we left

College and we ended up living not far from each other years later after we both migrated to Australia. Life went on and Mum received frequent letters from Dad full of loving words and telling her how much he missed her. He said he hated the army and couldn't wait to get home again.

At Christmas that year he expected a letter from Mum and when the post was delivered at the army camp in Egypt, all his colleagues had letters from their wives, girlfriends, and family but there wasn't one for him. Feeling pretty glum he was in the army mess when one of his mates came in, thumped him on the back, and handed him a letter from mum which he had held back to tease Dad!

 "Cheer up Robert," he said, "your wife hasn't forgotten you!" Dad was able to smile again.

During the next months, we received letters from Dad in one of which he promised to bring me a plane when he returned. I never got that plane. Then gradually his letters became fewer and fewer.

News of the progress of the war was regular. We heard a lot from the American soldiers who visited often. I remember one of them called Chilly Bean who was a lot of fun. He had the usual military close - cropped hair a cheerful round face and he was solidly built. He flirted outrageously with my cousin Moira, her mum Aunt Gwen keeping a watchful eye on them.

One afternoon one of them, not an American this time, named Joe decided to take me out to lunch at a local restaurant. We had a tasty tropical meal followed by a tub of ice cream and then it was time to pay. The waiter came up to me poker-faced and asked me to pay for my meal. I was paralysed with fear because I had no money. I said, "But I haven't any money."

He just looked at me and said, "You ate the meal and now you have to pay for it." I froze and looked appealingly at Joe. He just shrugged and I was just about to burst into tears when he said,

"It's okay we were just kidding," and he paid for the meal. I will never forget that. They may have thought it was funny but it terrified a little shy six-year-old kid with no father around to rescue him.

Now to what was happening in Europe.

The Battle of Normandy lasted from June to August 1944 and resulted in the Allied liberation of Western Europe from Nazi Germany's control. By late August 1944, all of northern France had been liberated and by the following spring, the Allies had defeated the Germans. The Normandy landings have been called the beginning of the end of the war in Europe.

With America and the Allied Forces fighting alongside each other, including the Canadians, the tide had turned inexorably.

In the three to four months to the end of April, the Allied forces took over 800,000 prisoners. German military leaders were facing the inevitable and Hitler committed suicide in his bunker at Berlin on 30 April 1945.

World War 2 ended with the unconditional surrender of the Axis powers. On 8 May 1945, the Allies accepted Germany's surrender about a week after Adolf Hitler had committed suicide

We were now living in a house opposite the British High Commission in Kandy. I remember the British flag being raised on its flagpole in the garden and the sounds of laughter and celebrations that went on late into the night.

The War was over! We would have our Dad back! We could hardly wait and were filled with excitement.

We waited, and waited.

But he never came back.

Chapter Three

Days turned into weeks, weeks into months and life had to go on.

I was progressing in school, Alex and Richard were next to be enrolled and Barbara was enrolled at a Convent School in Kandy.

One day Mum received a letter from Dad and she was crying as she read it.

She called us into her room and read it out to us. The part that sticks in our minds forever was when he wrote that he was to be de-mobbed from the army and he had requested it to happen in England. He was not coming back. He wrote, "If I were you I'd regard me as dead." Words that burned into Mum's and all our hearts.

We couldn't understand why and what was happening, but in hindsight, I guess Mum must have figured that he had met and fallen in love with someone else. It was heart-breaking. Here was Mum, post-war with four young children to raise. All I can say is thank God for family. Women did not regularly go out to work in the 1940s.

We were progressing in school and spent our school holidays with relatives – Aunt Edith in seaside Negombo, Aunt Daisy in Colombo, and Uncle Ric in whichever town he was stationed at as District Medical Officer and Chief Doctor of the town's Hospital.

The holidays at Uncle Ric's were the best. The first thing he would do when stationed at a new country town in a Government provided home was to build a tennis court and a swimming pool. He was a good tennis player, pianist, and ballroom dancer. He always kept beautiful gardens and often had a creek running through his property. There would be summer huts and bamboo bridges across the creek leading to them and pigeon cots. When he was transferred to a town called Watawala his house was on the side of a hill and he had terraced gardens down to the river at the bottom. Of course, he had gardeners and servants but he did pitch in and work alongside them. I remember them building a dam in the stream with rocks and fallen trees to make a natural swimming pool. We always had fun during those holidays. He had a Chevrolet convertible with an inbuilt picnic table attached to the back of the seat. He used to take us on picnics when he came home after his hospital rounds in the evenings. I have to thank him for all he did for me, for fostering my love of gardening and beautiful gardens. Something that has stayed with me until today.

He was an eccentric guy and had a rigid daily routine which he followed religiously.

He woke early and every morning at seven 'bed tea' would be brought in by a servant, a tray with tea, milk, and sugar laid on the bedside table for his first cup of tea for the day. Visitors would also be greeted every morning this way.

Then he would be in the garden till 8.30 supervising the gardeners and pitching in to help, mowing the lawns with an old Briggs and Stratton mower with its twisting blades which would clatter across the lawn spitting grass clippings behind it, filling the air with the smell of fresh-cut grass.

If we were on holiday with him we had to help with gardening duties every morning. He would also help with weeding, pruning, planting, and tidying up the beautiful gardens he loved to see maintained to a very high standard. His gardens, often terraced, always full of vivid colour, were a delight. Flowers like roses, chrysanthemums, dahlias, cosmos, coleus, caladiums (bleeding hearts), and salvia filled the garden with vivid colour, - reds, yellows, blues, and various hues in between.

I remember one morning with Alex and Richard standing in the garden, not knowing what he wanted us to do.

He had a short temper and said, "What are you doing boys? Don't just stand there, you can start by weeding this garden bed."

We hated to upset him because of his temper and we hadn't known what he wanted us to do.

So we replied,

"Yes, Uncle Ric," and got to work.

If we had started something on our own he would have yelled at us to do something else!

8.30 a.m. was his time to go into his 'music room' and play classical music on his grand piano. We were expected to sit quietly and 'appreciate the music.' We learned to like the compositions of Liszt, Brahms, Mozart, Strauss, and others.

Then he was off to do his ablutions and nine o'clock was breakfast time in the breakfast nook. This could either be traditional oats and toast, or the local hoppers (a pancake with a soft centre and delicious brown crust all around) with a local sambol (spicy coconut salad) and even local curries. All this washed down by a cup of famous Ceylon tea.

Next, he was off to do his hospital rounds and we had the place to ourselves. That's when we would explore his extensive property and climb the local hills.

He was back at noon for lunch, which would always be heralded by the ringing of the lunch gong. We would sometimes eat in the picnic area around the large fir tree on the lawn above the tennis court and sometimes in the dining room.

After lunch he would spend some time in his office attending to his correspondence, before sitting down to coffee and biscuits (always with a dash of salt in his coffee!) From two to four o'clock was his afternoon nap. We tried to stay clear of the house in the afternoons. At four he would wake up, get ready, and go on his afternoon hospital rounds.

Then he was back for afternoon tea which comprised scones, jam and cream, and sandwiches. Next, he played tennis till it started to get dark. He often invited friends over for tennis. He was a good tennis player but a sore loser.

After tennis, it was off for a shower and a time to relax before dinner. Dinner was at eight and again would be announced with the ringing of the dinner gong. Servants served at the dinner table and it always seemed semi-formal.

After dinner we would play board games and he would have his night time cup of tea, and then about nine he would invariably say, "I think it's time to retire," and it was off to bed for the night.

His routine never varied, and if we knew what was good for us we had to fit in with it. We soon got used to it and it was a small price to pay for the fun we had on holiday with him.

Sometimes we would go out for picnic lunches on the local grassland hills, or by a waterfall by the roadside, when we would have a dip in the cool mountain water at the foot of a waterfall.

There were times when we would have dinner at the picnic tables in his garden. It was never dull.

We would accompany him on the occasions when he went down to the local Tennis Club, of which he was a member where he won many a tennis trophy displayed in his trophy cabinet. We would play table tennis when we got the chance.

We looked forward to our holidays with Uncle Ric.

On 4th. February 1948 Ceylon, as it was then called, gained Independence from Britain and became the Dominion of Ceylon in the Commonwealth of Nations. A fledgling right-wing United National Party (UNP) held the reign of power at this time in Parliament.

I remember the Independence celebrations and the fireworks display over the Kandy Lake, as everyone felt pride and excited anticipation that we were now an independent nation.

The UNP had a large majority in Government and attracted a significant support base. There were, however, some basic weaknesses in the political structure. It was felt that the government represented only a small fraction of the population - the English-educated Westernized groups. To most of Sinhalese- and Tamil-educated citizens, these values appeared irrelevant. Unrest was brewing.

The island's three export products—tea, rubber, and coconuts—were succeeding in world markets, providing the majority of foreign exchange earnings.

However, the country began to face economic difficulties. A rapidly increasing population and the increasing import of consumer goods eroded earnings from foreign trade. The declining price of Ceylon's rubber and tea, and the increase in the price of imported food, added to the severe foreign exchange problem. Also, the expanded school system produced a large number of educated citizens who could not find employment.

My mother was determined to find her way and was successful in getting employment as a companion/housekeeper to a rich lady (Mrs. Dias) in a wealthy suburb in Colombo. We moved to Colombo to live with our grandparents in Quarry Road Dehiwela, a suburb of Colombo. Mum came over to spend the weekends with us.

Each Friday evening, when expecting Mum for her weekend visit, I would line up Barbara, Alex, and Richard and make them stand at attention at the front gate at the end of the driveway, to welcome Mum! They hated it and I don't know what made me do this. It must have been the influence of the War.

Dad and Mum -

The house in Kandy from where Dad left

Chapter Four

In 1950 my grandparents (Joe and Ethel) decided to migrate to Australia and submitted their application to the Australian High Commission in Colombo.

Grandad resigned his position as an architect at the local Council, sold their house in Dehiwela, and the house that he had built for my uncle George when their application to migrate was successful.

They wanted to take me with them, no doubt to ease Mum's burden. I even had my passport photo taken. I was not very happy because I could not bear the thought of being without Mum. First Dad and then Mum? No way! I made my feelings known in no uncertain manner (I may have even turned on a tantrum, I can't remember) I am sure Mum would have felt a pang at losing me, although she knew it was in her best interests. I loved my Grandad and Ma but I loved my Mum more! In any event, I wasn't with them when they left for Melbourne with my uncles Lanny and George, his wife Patricia, their two sons, Chris and Tony, and daughters Cheryl and Lorraine. My uncle John had preceded them a few months before they left.

My Aunt Marie had married Jock, who was in the British Navy and had already moved to Scotland. Marie and Jock had four children - Ben (born in Sri Lanka), Michael (born in England), Peter (born in Malta), and Pam (born in Australia). She joked that whenever Jock was moved by the Navy to a different country she became pregnant.

I often wonder how my life would have turned out had I migrated with them when I was thirteen. It was a life-changing moment when the decision was made for me, but in light of how the rest of my life has panned out, it was the right one. I wouldn't change some of the best years of my life for anything.

For the two years I lived with Ma and Grandad in Colombo I attended a local school, St. Mary's, doing well and scoring good grades. I was amused when looking through my 'Baby Book' one day, kept by Mum noting my progress from birth, with notes on my first words, cutting my first tooth, first steps, and other milestones. I came across an entry that said, 'Awarded prize for the Best Citizen in the school empire at St. Mary's.' It was just a primary school. I recall it here because it was such an unusual title for a school award.

While at St. Mary's I befriended a classmate named Ramchand. He was a fair-skinned curly-headed boy who kept to himself most of the time and did not seem to have many friends. We became good pals and hung together during school breaks and walked home together when school was out.

Our other classmates seemed to resent our friendship and did their best to cause friction between us.

Friends sometimes fell out with each other. There was a ritual when two friends wanted to end their friendship, where they would extend their hands in a handshake and get someone to bring his open hand down on theirs and 'cut' the friendship. They would then stay away from each other until one day they would decide to be friends again and repeat this ritual, 'cutting' their separation, so they could be friends again.

Classmates decided it was time to drive a wedge between Ramchand and me. They told me that Ramchand was spreading lies about me, and him that I was 'bad-mouthing' him to others.

They told each of us that we shouldn't be friends. It finally got to us and though we didn't realise it at the time, one day a mutual friend, Bernie, manipulated the ending of our mateship.

When we were together, he cut us angry which was the accepted term for ending a friendship. For the next couple of days, we avoided each other but I was uneasy as I knew I had not 'bad-mouthed' Ramchand and I didn't believe he would have spread lies about me.

So-called friends then started to goad us to fight, saying things like, "Don't let him get the better of you, you have to teach him a lesson."

One afternoon after school was out we were in a group and Ramchand and I found ourselves opposite each other with many of our classmates around us in a circle, goading us to fight.

One of the guys, Rohan said, "Go on, and give it to him, Ramchand."

Another, Sunil said, "Do it, Robert, show us that you can fight."

We ended up facing off, our fists raised in front of us like boxers, circling each other. We feinted and kept moving, taking tentative pokes at each other, neither of us landing a blow. I looked at Ramchand and thought,

'I've really got nothing against you, and I just can't do this.' His eyes told me the same from his end.

But the kids in the circle kept up a chant. "Go! Go! Go! Let's see what you've got!"

He finally shot out his fist, landing a glancing blow on my cheek. I answered with a feeble counter to his jaw which caught him by surprise, but I winced as I connected. Neither of us wanted to continue, and we feinted and circled each other. No further blows were attempted and the kids around us realised that they were not going to get the entertainment they were expecting and gradually dispersed.

That left the two of us. We just looked at each other and said "Sorry," at the same time.

I repeated, "Sorry, Ramchand, friends?" He nodded, and we both teared up as we hugged and talked about what had happened.

We realised that we had been set up and none of what we heard about each other was true. It was with a great sense of relief that we walked home together, as we both had felt miserable all week.

I was in for a surprise though when I reached home. My Grandma greeted me at the door sternly, "Roger! What have you been up to? I hear you've fought with some kid." She sat me down on the living room couch and took a chair opposite me and said, "Now tell me what happened."

"I'm sorry Ma, I didn't mean to". And I went on to explain what had happened. She listened patiently to what I had to say and gave me some good advice.

She said, "Son, never believe everything you hear, especially if you think it's not true. Trust your gut, more often than not it is right."

I still don't know how she heard about this incident as I came straight home with Ramchand after it was over.

You may wonder why she called me Roger. That's another story! When I was born Mum and Dad wanted to name me Roger. When it came to my baptism, as we were Catholics, the priest told them they had to give me a saint's name. They couldn't find Roger in their record of saints' names, so they chose Robert, the same name as my father. I was always called Roger at home, but in school and everywhere else I was Robert.

At that time we had the only 'radiogram' in the street. It was a large cabinet one side of which there was a radio, and the other a turntable. One day my brother Alex, curious to see who was talking on the radio, sneaked in behind the cabinet and tried to get inside, to see who was there. He ended up getting an electric shock, and never went looking again.

Chapter Five

My uncles John and Lanny were in their late teens at this time. Lanny was the youngest in the family. John was of medium height, with brown wavy hair and medium build. Lanny was taller, slimmer, also with dark wavy hair and a mischievous glint in his blue eyes. He was the more handsome of the two.

One evening they had been flirting with two neighbouring sisters, Kathy and Annette, Kathy was the older of the two. She was a fraction taller than the five foot six Annette. Slim, with attractive hazel eyes, she was a brunette like her sister. She had shoulder-length hair, whereas Annette's hair was closely cropped around a 'baby' face. Annette could hardly be described as 'plump' but she had a fuller figure than Kathy. Annette's brown eyes had a pensive look about them. The sisters were sitting on the low wall on their porch next door, swinging their legs back and forth, exchanging glances and unspoken signals with the brothers next door. The dividing fence between the two properties was a low one and the two houses were close enough for conversation between the neighbours. Kathy wore a plain blue cotton skirt and a white silk top that hugged her curves, of which she was fully aware. Annette was in a faded pair of black cotton shorts and a sleeveless yellow top.

Kathy caught Lanny's glance and she flirtatiously flicked her hair over her shoulder. Lanny winked back at her and motioned with his hand for her to stay there as he went into the sitting room. He could play some chords on the piano and he was playing and singing the song "I'll take you home again, Kathleen" when their parents called them in and the family went out soon after.

The two brothers were feeling bored. They decided to raid their other next-door neighbour's Jak fruit tree.

Jak fruit trees have a thick trunk and grow thirty to forty feet high. They have a dark green canopy of spirally arranged leaves, shaped somewhat like liquid amber but much larger. The fruit on the tree resembled large green melons with a spiky thick outer skin. The ripened fruit can be sliced open to reveal a bulb of flowers attached to a central stalk. The petals are thick, yellow, and packed together down the stalk filling the inside of the fruit. They are edible, have a sweet smell, and taste like a combination of apple, pineapple, and mango. Jak fruit are high in potassium, protein, and vitamin B. The seeds inside the fleshy inflorescence can be roasted, boiled, or baked and eaten.

The two boys went out the back of their house and Lanny said, "I'll get the ladder from the shed." John peeped over the back fence, which was higher than the one in front of the house at six feet, looked around his neighbour's yard, and announced, "Coast clear let's get this done."

Lanny brought the ladder out and they hoisted it over the fence, which the two of them then scaled, landing on the other side next to the ladder. "Oops!" exclaimed John, "Forgot the rope," and he had to clamber back over the fence to get a length of rope from the shed. Lanny placed the ladder against the tree and John came back with the coiled rope slung over his head, resting on his shoulder. Making no noise John climbed the ladder, the top resting just below the first two fruit, which grew on stems off the bark of the tree. He could tell by the smell that the fruit was ripe and ready to be eaten.

"Damn!" he whispered, "The knife!" They'd forgotten the knife.

Lanny went back to get the knife as John came down to the base of the ladder. Taking the knife between his teeth he went up the ladder again and cut the stem of one of the fruits, which he grabbed awkwardly, leaning against the tree as he tied the Jak fruit by the stem and lowered it down to Lanny. Lanny untied the fruit, went over to the fence, and dropped the jack fruit down on their side of the fence.

It fell with a thud, and the boys froze for a minute. All was quiet and John, who had the other end of the rope attached to his belt, started slicing away at the stem of the second Jak fruit. Lanny was waiting at the bottom of the ladder. John had almost sliced the stem through when it happened!

Their neighbour Alfonso came yelling out of his house. "Hey! Whatsa going on? You boys stealing my fruit? Stay where you are. You going to get a pissa my temper now!"

Lanny took one look at an angry man bearing down on them and wasted no time in hastily clambering over the fence, leaving John to face the music, caught red-handed with the Jak fruit in his hands.

Lanny bolted into his room, chuckling that he had got away in time, but feeling bad that he had left John holding the baby, or Jak fruit in this case.

"Aw," he said to himself, "John would have done the same to me I'm sure."

A few minutes later John came in nursing a sore backside. He was furious at Lanny.

"Nice one bro," he said, "Left me holding the candle, didn't you? Didn't expect that of you. Nice brother to have. You could have waited and faced the music with me. Maybe I should give you a taste of what I got, teach you a bit about loyalty."

Lanny came back with, "I'm sorry John, but come on, you would have done the same to me."

"Maybe I would, we'll never know, but now we've got the problem of getting the ladder back. Old Alfonso wants us to come over with Dad and an apology if we want the ladder back."

"Shit, we're both going to cop it from Dad now," Lanny said.

"Yes, and I cop two punishments to your one," John replied.

They didn't look forward to their encounter with their father because they knew how strict he was.

John said, "At least we got a Jak fruit out of it. Maybe we can negotiate with Alfonso, - tell him he had a ripe Jak fruit which he didn't have to climb the tree for."

"You really think that's going to cut it?" Lanny said despondently.

"You're right," said John, "he's probably going to ask if we took any fruit ourselves."

"What are we going to say?"

"If we say yes, he'll want the fruit for himself. He'll ask us to give it back. And Dad will make sure we do."

"We're going to have sore backsides anyway – a second one for you. We better say no. We'll have to keep the fruit for ourselves. Probably get sick from eating it all."

John said, "What about the smell? Mum will know there's a Jak fruit in the house. Shit, we're stuffed. Shouldn't have done it Who's idea was it anyway?"

"Doesn't matter," said Lanny, "We're stuck with it now. We better wrap it up and hide it in the shed, Hope Mum or Dad don't go in there for a couple of days."

Moral of the story - don't get caught stealing your neighbour's fruit!

Chapter Six

After my grandparents left for a new life in Australia we moved back to Aunt Gwen's home in Kandy. My uncle Willie had been appointed Acting Principal of Kingswood College and occupied the Principal's residence on the school property. We were there for two years. Living on the school premises we never had to worry about being late for classes. I became interested in cricket and we always had a cricket match going, sometimes continuing from one break to the next.

At the end of Uncle Willie's stint as Acting Principal we moved to another house on the main Colombo-Kandy Road, about half a mile away.

Kingswood was founded by Louis Edmond Blaze, a remarkable educator ahead of his time. It encompassed primary and secondary education on the same premises, in different blocks, up to University Entrance. His passion was to educate his pupils not merely to achieve academic success. He strove in all his teaching - and imparted it on his staff, to produce not only scholars but gentlemen.

Each morning at the school assembly he addressed staff and pupils thus, "Good morning ladies and gentlemen, and gentlemen of Kingswood." You can imagine what that made us, his pupils, feel. We felt special and privileged, and being addressed in this way instilled in us the desire to live up to his expectations. The school had a unique ambience that commanded loyalty and ethos that stayed with pupils long after their school days were over. There were about a thousand pupils in the school from diverse backgrounds – Christians of different denominations, Buddhists. Muslims, and Hindus in the main. We celebrated Christmas and Easter and our Buddhist and Muslim friends mingled with us at these times. We celebrated Buddhist festivals like Vesak, and Poson (significant full moon festivals), and Ramadan – a month of intense prayer and dawn to dusk fasting for Muslims. Everyone joined in and respected everyone else's customs beliefs and practices. We celebrated the Gregorian calendar New Year, Sinhalese New Year, the Kandy Perahera (a spectacular Buddhist pageant of a procession of elephants, dancers, drummers, and whip crackers) Deepavali and Katagarama Peraheras (Hindu processions), and other non-religious festivals like Independence Day.

Everybody joined in the fun and frivolity of these events and enjoyed the various foods served on these occasions. No one was offended. No one had anything to protest about.

One can only imagine a world where this is the norm.

Kingswood's founder Louis Blaze composed the School Song. It is the most inspiring school song I have heard and I include it here. I will preface this by saying Kingswood was built on a hill in the heart of Kandy.

We sang it regularly at the school assembly, and by repetition, sub-consciously committed it to memory.

The Kingswood Song

Hill throned, where nature is gracious and kind,

Home of our early youth – grant us the love of truth,

Health for the body and light for the mind.

Kingswood O may we loyal and true to thee,

Holding what e'er betide, Virtue and Faith our guide.

Chorus.

Loyally, manfully all of us true to thee,

No room for trimmer, coward or fool,

Word and will true and clean

Work and play, strong and keen

None for himself but all for the school,

School, School, none for himself but all, ALL for the school.

Nor shall the world destroy our love and pride,

For both, we know, the stronger shall grow,

And whatever thy fortune we stand at thy side.

Present and past shall be one in heart all for thee,

Holding what e'er betide, Virtue and Faith our guide.

Chorus.

Then in all things wherever Duty's voice may call,

Ready we follow and spring to our work,

Country or School may call, Play the game. Forward all!

Shoulder to shoulder, disdaining to shirk!

Duty we dare not flee, heavy the cost may be,

Holding what e'er betide, Virtue and Faith our guide.
Chorus

Once they reached secondary school students were divided into four 'houses' vying for academic and sporting honours represented by the Randles and Crowther Shields donated by generous benefactors. Built on British tradition the houses were Eton, Harrow, Rugby, and Winchester. I was allotted to Harrow, Alex to Rugby, and Richard to Winchester.

We represented our respective houses in cricket, soccer, hockey, and athletics. I also represented Kingswood at cricket in the Inter-school competition.

My good friend Derrick was appointed captain of Winchester, Nissanka – Eton, Jumar – Rugby and I was captain of Harrow. Competition between us was keen but fair. Harrow was fortunate one year to win both the

Randles and Crowther Shields. For the Randles Shield points were allotted based on students' academic achievement.

We also participated in Inter-House Debates and Plays, joined the Scouts, and then the Rover Scouts. We received a well-rounded education and will always fondly remember our school days.

School Prefects were nominated by House Masters each year to replace those that had ended their school careers. Prefects were the bridge between students and teachers and had some responsibility in maintaining discipline. Too much, we felt at times.

For instance, students were forbidden from going to the cinema during the week and prefects helped police this restriction. Yes, times were different then.

One Wednesday my good friend George and I decided to defy this rule - which we considered stupid - and hurried down after school to the Regal Cinema, a stone's throw from where I lived. We just caught the matinee screening of 'Captain Horatio Hornblower.' We bought the cheapest tickets to the 'gallery' – the section closest to the screen.

"Hey! George, come over here," I said, "I don't think there's a Prefect here today, have you seen anyone?" "Nope." he replied, "We could be lucky." We felt uneasy though because we were breaking a rule.

The next morning at break time one of the prefects, Asoka, summoned us to the library which was where they hung out.

"And where were you two last afternoon about 3.30?" he asked, and we knew we had been sprung.

"You were at the movies," he said. "You knew you were breaking the rules."

We didn't say anything, looking down sheepishly. He tipped my chin up with his left hand and slapped me hard on the left cheek with his right hand. Then it was George's turn and we had paid the price for our indiscretion. We figured they had been in the mid-section of the cinema.

When I became a prefect I never laid a hand on another student as I and my peers at that time thought it was inappropriate.

After the island gained independence the Government decided it was time to move away from British colonial influence and introduced Sinhalese as the official State language. Students were now to be taught in Sinhalese; the only exception to this rule was students whose mother tongue was English. A Sinhalese Examination Paper was however mandatory for Senior School Certificate qualification. We were able to continue our education in the English Stream but I had to score a pass in "Sinhalese Language" to qualify for my Senior School Certificate. I could speak Sinhalese, lots of my friends being Sinhalese, but the spoken and written word had different rules and I found this difficult to cope with. To speak with one set of rules and write to another set just didn't make sense to me. Once in my Sinhalese class we were set an assignment, which I completed. When all our assignments had been assessed, the Sinhalese master read mine out to the class, as an example of how *not* to do an assignment. I was understandably pissed off I think and stopped trying. Had he taken me aside and tried to help me improve, the result may have been different.

Some of my 'English speaking' friends succeeded but although I passed all my other subjects well, I never mastered Sinhalese. I did not pass my Senior School Certificate examination although I spent a year in the University Entrance Class, while I re-sat my entire exam. With the same results. This did not have an impact on my employment prospects.

Chapter Seven

When we moved back to Kandy Mum applied for - and was successful in securing - a job at Kandy Girls' High School, running the cafeteria. She ended her employment with Mrs. Dias in Colombo and moved in with Aunt Gwen in Kandy. Mrs. Dias was sorry to see her go but appreciated her need to be with her children.

"I have loved having you look after things for me my dear, but I can understand your needs at this time. I hope you are happy in your new job and wish you nothing but the best," she said as she gave mum a goodbye hug.

"Thank you for taking me on when I needed the work. I have enjoyed working for you and I hope you find a replacement soon," my Mum said and left to catch the bus to take her to Kandy.

Mum was everything to us and we wouldn't allow anyone to do or say anything to hurt her. They would have had to reckon with us and we always had Mum's back, as she always had ours. We may not have had much when we were growing up but we had the love of an amazing mother, a roof over our heads, food in our stomachs, and clothes on our backs. We didn't ask for more. We had all we needed and life was good.

Not many had phones at home at that time. If we needed to make a call we had to go to the Post Office. Out of area was a trunk call. We had to book a call and the Post Office would give us a time, usually hours later, when we would have to go back to make the call. Eating at a restaurant was a special treat. A good lunch was curry and rice. Ice-cream was a treat on a hot day.

When we were sent to the butchers to buy meat for dinner, the butcher's meat was hung on hooks in the open. With flies buzzing around, he sliced the meat off the bone and wrapped it in an old newspaper, while buses belched smoke on the road just outside. We hardly ever got sick and all this exposure built up some strong immune systems.

We took our school clothes off as soon as we got home and put on our play clothes. We had to do our homework before being allowed outside to play. The family always ate dinner at the table.

There was no TV and a Rediffusion set was a box fixed to the wall with four pre-set radio stations for news and music. We played cricket in the garden, hop-scotch, Hide and Seek, Cowboys and Crooks, Truth or Dare and Dodge ball. Staying in the house was a punishment and we were never bored.

We ate what was cooked for us – and there was no bottled water.

We never imagined the day would come when we would have to pay for water.

We listened to "Sunday Choice" in the afternoons hoping our choice, sent in by mail would be played.

We rode our bikes for hours, with no helmet or safety gear. On weekends we went out in the morning with a picnic lunch and returned in the evening.

We weren't afraid of anything and played till dark. Sunset as our curfew.

Attendance at school was mandatory and teachers were people we could trust and respect.

We were never allowed to talk back to our elders. Our family were our best friends. When we went out to play with friends we just turned up at their front door and yelled their names to come out and play. I remember trying to yell the name 'Lytton' out loud. It was impossible! Those were the good old days and I wouldn't trade them for anything.

As far as boundaries were concerned I don't remember Mum setting any; it was left to our common sense and we did not let her down.

Chapter Eight

Those years in Kingswood were some of the best years of my life. It was where I learned so much both academically and also about the 'school of life'. About living together with people of diverse backgrounds, beliefs, and customs. Being part of a common goal, being part of a community with compassion and loyalty and helping each other when help was needed. They were defining, never to be forgotten years, that shaped us and prepared us for life after school and college. And we have the founder of Kingswood, Louis Edmond Blaze, to thank for that. For it was his vision and philosophy that drove his staff to follow and spread his ideals and wisdom that helped shape us from the boys we were to the men we are.

It was my Physics and Scout Master, Anton Blacker, who fostered my love of nature, open spaces, and love of adventure. The scout camps he took us on were full of action and excitement. We were in Patrols and had to keep our sites spick and span for inspection each morning at dawn. After physical training exercises and breakfast cooked by us, he would set trails that we had to follow, looking for broken twigs on branches that formed part of the trail, or three stones one on top of the other graded according to size signifying water close by, to give you two examples.

I remember once up in the mountains during the camp our scout group hiked over 50 kilometres in the jungle to our destination and back, looking for a place called Nitre Cave, said to be infested by flying foxes. Its name is said to have derived from the phosphorous glow, caused by the aging of droppings left by the large numbers of flying foxes inhabiting the cave.

Another time an exercise was our group having to hike across a valley at dusk to a mountain across from our camp-site and having to signal back in Morse code with a flashlight, that we had reached our destination. The call-up sign was VE in Morse code. – Dot, dot, dot, dash (V) then Dot (E). This was signalled with three short flashes of the flashlight, followed by a longer flash (for V) and a single short flash (for E)

. . . ____ **(V)**

. **(E)**

So we had to repeat . . . ____   .   . . . ____ .

We finally had an answer from the base camp that they were receiving our signal. One of the scouts said to Ashley, who carried the flashlight, "Careful now, don't make a mistake or the message will get scrambled."

"Don't worry," replied Ashley, "I'm being careful."

The signalling went all right, was received at base camp and we got the message, "Dinner's ready. Come and get it."

We replied, "On the way – over and out," and headed back down the valley. We had to role play that one of us was injured and had to be carried on an improvised stretcher and that someone was me.

Anton Blacker taught me a harsh lesson in discipline. I was the Co-editor of the College magazine – an annual booklet summarising the year with articles by House Captains, the Principal's Annual Report delivered on Prize-Giving day, the Chief Guest's speech, and details of the Annual Prize Giving for academic and sports achievements. It also contained articles of interest submitted by students and reports from various school associations. The editors had to travel by bus to the city after school was out to progressively proof-read the publication. My co-editor and I took it in turns to do this. Andrew, my co-editor was lazy and kept missing his turn at the printer. So I had to go in to do most of the proof-reading.

As a result, I had attended two scout meetings that semester, one short of the required three to qualify to go on the annual scout camp in the central mountains. My name was not on the list of attendees.

I appealed to the Senior Scout Group Committee, headed by Anton Blacker because my duties as co-editor had made me miss that third scout meeting. After my appeal was considered I was informed that a rule was a rule. I had broken the rule and I was not able to be included in the camp. I was devastated as I had been so looking forward to it.

To make things worse I had to help pack the trailer with camping supplies, push it to the railway station to be loaded onto the train, and wave goodbye as the train pulled out of the station.

Years later, in Australia, I said a few words in a speech on the occasion of Anton's 90th birthday and reminded him of the lesson he had taught me on discipline. He winced.

Then there was L.B. Fernando. The school day commenced each morning with two assemblies, one for Christians and one for non- Christians. It was no big deal. It was just common sense. If you were a Christian you attended the Christian assembly. If you weren't, you attended the Non-Christian assembly. L.B. was the schoolmaster who at Non-Christian assembly one morning, said, "The Gogerly boys are destroying nature."

We could have been the butt of criticism from other students, but we weren't. The lesson we learnt? Not to take notice of idiots!

A few weeks later we entered our collection in a Hobbies Exhibition and were awarded First Prize. "Up yours!" L.B. Fernando, we thought.

There was also Sydney Perera, our Geography and English Literature teacher. He was also my House Master. He fostered my interest in Geography and exploration - our love of hiking and open spaces. It was this that led to my best friend Ashley and me creating a bathymetric map of the Kandy Lake showing the relief on the lake bed. We hiked all the mountains around our home town – Kandy. He took us on excursions, showing us where tributaries of streams converged to form a river, which meandered its way down a valley forming eddies as it flowed down to a delta and into the sea. He took us to wild-life sanctuaries where we saw leopards, wild elephants, bears, crocodiles, and beautifully coloured birds in their natural habitat.

In a country small enough that distance was no hindrance to viewing these aspects of nature on day trips or short overnighters, it made our learning inexpensive and so much fun outdoors as well as in the confines of a classroom.

He also taught us English Literature and spiked my interest in Shakespeare, the classics, and acting. He produced plays in which I acted and supported our participation in inter-house debates, mock court trials, and Parliamentary sessions.

He selected me to represent the school at the National Schools Radio Reading and Recitation Competition at which I was Runner-up. I skipped a rehearsal once and was hauled to the Principal's office for a caning.

The lesson? When you are given a responsibility – take it seriously.

To say our school days were idyllic would not be an exaggeration.

Chapter Nine

Trincomalee, with one of the largest natural harbours in the world, lies in the north-east corner of Sri Lanka. It was a British naval base because of its strategic position in the Indian Ocean.

Set on a rocky outcrop called Swami Rock in a peninsular in the north of Trincomalee, Fort Frederick was built by the Portuguese in the 16th century. It was dismantled and rebuilt by the Dutch in 1665.

Remnants of the past, cannons, and artillery are now dotted around the fort, A small number of spotted deer graze under huge banyan trees in the compound.

Hidden away on a cliff in Swami Rock lies another rocky outcrop which is called Lovers' Leap. Legend has it that it got its name from a well- known story about a woman named Francine who was engaged to a

Dutch officer who broke off their engagement, broke her heart, and left her to go back to his homeland of Holland. As she watched the sailing ship he was on leave Trincomalee she walked up to this vantage point and threw herself into the ocean as the ship sailed past, heartbroken and devastated, unable to face life alone.

Uncle Ric was posted to Trincomalee for a stint as District Medical Officer and Chief Doctor of the town hospital. We waited impatiently to spend a school holiday there. Finally, the day arrived for the start of the vacation at the end of the semester, and he picked us up in his convertible Chevrolet and drove the 180 kilometres between Kandy in the hills and his house in Trincomalee on the coast.

The beach was not far from his house and it was not long before we were frolicking in the waves and picking oysters off the rocks close to the shore. At night we sometimes went down to the fishermen's boats resting in a row on the sand and climbed inside to sleep under the stars. No one seemed to mind. It was uncomfortable on the floor of the boat, but it was a small price to pay for falling asleep under a canopy of bright twinkling stars bathed by the dreamy light of a full moon, lulled to sleep by the sound of waves breaking on the shore.

Stop for a moment, close your eyes, and listen. Can you hear it? We would occasionally see a shooting star streaking across the sky as we drifted off to sleep.

I remember one occasion when we did this. The four of us brothers and our sister were between twelve and sixteen years old. We were accompanied by Uncle Ric.

The arrival of the fishermen about 3 a.m. woke us from our dreams and we had to give up our beds for the night. The smell of the salty sea air assailed our nostrils as we stretched awake. The fishermen went out in two rows on either side of a vast net, rowing out into the sea spreading their net as they went. It was time for us to head back home to our beds to finish our night's sleep.

Then we woke at dawn and hurried down to the beach again. We could see the top of the nets, wooden floats attached to it, bobbing up and down in the waves, the net was spread below the surface to trap their catch of fish for the day. The fishermen lined up on two sides of the beach and started hauling in the huge net. They chanted as they pulled in a halting rhythm, as each float reached their hands and they laid it with the net on the beach.

They swayed forward and back with each chant. One row chanted loud and clear, "O de elei!" The other row would respond, "Elei yah!"

"O de elei"

"Elei yah!"

"O de elei"

"Elei yah!"

Then the chanting got louder and changed to

"ELEI - ELEI"

"ELEI - ELEI"

"ELEI – ELEI"

"ELEI – YAH."

The net was gradually dragged in as the sun rose seemingly lazily in the brisk morning air. Seagulls began circling above, calling out their cry of 'Karr, Karr, Karr' anticipating a morning meal of freshly caught fish. Little fisher folk children straggled onto the beach in scantily clad colourful clothes rubbing their sleepy eyes with the back of their knuckles, to watch their fathers, as entranced as we were at the ritualistic haul.

As the net piled up on the two sides of the beach, the end of the net was pulled in from the sea and began to appear, and silvery flashes of frantically leaping fish appeared.

Closer and closer the end was hauled up onto the beach. The murmur amongst the fishermen grew louder and louder as they were able to identify the fish in their haul and point out the tuna, trevally, mackerel, and mullet.

On this morning the catch of the day happened to be two red Snapper called 'thabalayaa' in Sinhalese. Ecstatic screams of, "THABALAYAA" rent the air, as they gathered around the net, now completely ashore. It was a good catch, and the excitement and anticipation of good sales at the fish market became evident in the chatter and laughter amongst the fishermen. The smell of the fish mingled with the salty smell of the sea.

Then it was time to divide the haul amongst themselves and haggle over who would get the thabalayaa, and negotiate the trade-offs.

They carried their catch in two large baskets attached to a long pole at each end, slung over their shoulder, and headed off to the market to start a new day.
Life was good.

My cousin Paddy, her husband Anton McHeyzer and their four children were also in Trincomalee at this time. Anton was the Government Agent at Trincomalee and had a beautiful house on the top of a hill overlooking a cove aptly named Sandy Cove. A private beach.

A row of stone steps led down to the beach from their house, where we were frequent visitors during our vacation.

We spent hours exploring the beach, collecting seashells, frolicking amongst the rocks at the water's edge, and delving into the jungle bordering the steps.

Paddy was a buxom brunette with bright blue eyes, short wavy hair, and a full rounded figure. Anton was tall, well built, with grey eyes - which were a feature of his face - and wore glasses. He had a receding hairline and his full head of hair was flecked with grey at the temples. He was a well-known Rugby Union player with the Havelock's, a prominent club in Colombo in the Rugby Football Tournament.

One day he was working under his car - a black Holden sedan - installing a new muffler. His hand slipped when tightening a nut and the muffler crashed down on his face smashing his glasses, sending a splinter into his eye. He was rushed to the hospital where he underwent surgery but was never able to play Rugby football again.

They were not able to remove the tiny splinter in his eye and he had to live with it for the rest of his life.

The recently crowned Queen Elizabeth 11 of England was visiting Sri Lanka (still Ceylon at the time) on her first visit to the new independent Dominion of Ceylon. She was due to visit the naval base at Trincomalee, and Anton (as Government Agent), and family were to host her for afternoon tea at his property.

There was great excitement at the McHeyzer household at the prospect of meeting the Queen. Anton spent a tidy sum re-laying the front lawn and hired a gardener to spruce up and tidy the property for the visit. The kids had new clothes bought for them and they were all looking forward to the day with keen anticipation.

Then, at the last minute, the visit to Trincomalee was cancelled, and a reception in the capital of Colombo was scheduled in its place.

Everyone felt disappointed and 'flat'.

I was an avid cricket fan. A Test series of matches between England and Australia was taking place in England. At night when everyone had gone to bed, I quietly made my way into the living room to the house radio, in a large cabinet much like the one at my grandparent's house. I switched it on, turned the volume down low so as not to disturb anyone, and tuned in to listen to the commentary on the game. I was soon engrossed in the progress of the match.

Then I heard a sound that froze me with fear.

I heard footsteps on the veranda outside. The house was in darkness and there was a watery moon shedding pale light on the garden, the shadowy trees swaying in the breeze. I have a vivid imagination and I imagined Portuguese and Dutch soldiers in armour in days of old as they patrolled the streets of the town. I stayed very still. There it was again. A kind of swish, swish, the sound of heavy squashy footsteps on the veranda outside.

Was it a ghost? Can ghosts make noise? My hackles rose as I listened intently.

Silence.

A wicket fell in the cricket match and I was drawn back to the commentary. I felt something soft brush against my bare leg (I was in boxer shorts) and my heart nearly stopped beating. Then I heard a purr and realised it was the cat.

Back came the footsteps, smooth, deliberate, slow. Swish, swish, swish, swish.

My heart was thumping in me and I was sweating.

After a short pause, it was back, furtive, and stealthy. Swish, swish. I couldn't move. I was now scared out of my wits. I imagined the ghost of a soldier, Portuguese or Dutch, walking outside.

I gathered up my courage and crept towards my room.

Then, in the dim light of the moon coming from outside, I saw the curtains swaying in the breeze coming in through the open windows. The bottom of the curtain was brushing against the linoleum on the floor making this swishing noise as it moved back and forth in the breeze.

Swish, swish, back and forth, fanned by the breeze. Swish, swish, swish, swish.

I had found my ghost!

———————————————————————

Ta-Da! . . . Drum Roll . . .

Sequel to this memory. Fast forward . . .

Real-time, 20 June 2020.

I had a dream!

We were in our garden, in Dingley Village on the front lawn under a fruit tree (which isn't there). It had a thick bark lush green foliage and was laden with pink pear-shaped fruit. I was with Jan and a small child. It was late evening and almost dark. Then suddenly we became aware of a Japanese woman on our driveway about twenty metres away. We sensed that she was dangerous and evil. She carried a sword and crouching, scanned the garden looking for us. She couldn't see us in the dim light, behind the tree. We saw her scurry down the right side of the house looking for us.

We had our backs to the road outside and were facing the front of the house. We crouched down behind the bark of the tree and waited apprehensively. I was on my haunches and Jan lay against my back her chin tucked in between my neck and shoulder. The kid was at my feet. We stayed motionless not wanting to give our position away.

Then I heard the sound of something being bumped into on our left, and I sensed that she had come out the front on the left side of the house. It was dark now and we couldn't see her. Jan had fallen asleep on my shoulder.

Then she started to hiss, to scare us no doubt. The hissing became louder. My heart thumped in my chest as I tried to move but couldn't because of the weight of Jan. I tried to nudge Jan off my shoulder but she wouldn't wake up.

The hissing became even louder and closer. I had to do something but was trapped under Jan's weight. Fear gripped me and I whispered to Jan, "Wake up, she's here and we've got to act." Still no response. The hissing was very close now and I was getting desperate.

 All I had was a dagger in my right hand with a foot-long blade. (This happens in dreams!)

I was scared, trapped, and terrified, and did the only thing I could – I let out a blood-curdling scream!

The thing was I yelled right into Jan's ear and she sat bolt upright in bed, instantly awake. "What's wrong, what's wrong?" And I told her about what happened.

Scared the cat (who was sleeping on the bed) right out of its wits as it streaked through the door out of the room like a bat out of hell.

Okay, you can stop laughing now!

Back to My Story . . .

Chapter Ten

Our friends Robin and Bernard D'Abrera lived just a short distance from us in Kandy on the opposite side of the main Colombo-Kandy road, at Primrose Hill.

Their father was the Pathologist at the Kandy Hospital. They had a large house at the end of a winding driveway with a yard on both sides, where we used to play cricket with them. The family included their mother and younger sisters Maryann and Imogen.

Robin was my age, solidly built with dark hair, a square jaw, and wore glasses. Bernard was a year younger, slim, with a wiry build, and slightly curly hair, and with an outgoing nature. Robin was the more reserved of the two. We didn't see much of Maryann or Imogen who always seemed to have girl-friends around.

We were frequent visitors to their home and one day while visiting we spent some time looking through a book from their father's library – "The Butterfly Fauna of Ceylon" written by L .G. O. Woodhouse an eminent lepidopterist.

We spread the book on the large dining table, sitting around it as Robin read.

We were intrigued by the beautiful illustrations of the two hundred and forty-two species of butterflies in Ceylon. Interesting too was how the different species were classified into 'families' according to their nomenclature, migratory habits, size, the shape of their wings, and other characteristics. Their different life histories fascinated us. We read how the female butterfly would lay her eggs underneath the leaves of the only food plant that her species survived on. Of the myriad plants in forests and gardens, she would unerringly pick the correct one for her caterpillars to eat once they hatched out of their eggs. When the caterpillars ate the leaves and grew, they would moult out of their skins several times before the next stage of their lives. Some of them extended spongy horns which exuded an unpleasant scent when they sensed predators close-by ready to feed on them. This deterred them from approaching.

In one species ants would protect the caterpillars in their nest, in exchange for sweet secretions provided by the caterpillars for the ants to feed on. A perfect lesson in peaceful co-existence.

"Wow!" Richard exclaimed. "I didn't know that insects had intelligence." That was the day we all became amateur lepidopterists and started our butterfly collections. Needless to say, this soon developed into a competition between the three Gogerly brothers and the two D'Abrera's.

The butterflies on the island were divided into very common, common, not rare, rare, and very rare. We started with the very common and common varieties. We used the handles of old brooms to which we attached a round hoop and netting, which we sewed onto the hoop, to complete our home-made butterfly nets.

Each time we caught a new species we would refer to the book to identify it, before we stored it in wooden cases which we made. The butterflies had to be 'set' to expand their four wings, so their full colours could be displayed as they were pinned in the boxes. The boxes needed to be air-tight,

As our collections swelled from the very common to common we went searching for the not rare and rarer varieties, which were harder to find. Each time we caught a new species to add to our collection we would hang out sometimes for up to an hour, waiting for another specimen to appear. Robin and Bernard would want to know where these new species were caught, as we wanted to know where they captured new species as well. There came a time when the competition was hotting up when each of us would give the other the wrong location and both parties would hang around for ages with no success.

The butterflies in the tropics are very bright and colourful with different patterns, wing sizes, and shapes. They have different modes of flight – some zippy and swift, others slow and lazy. Some fly low and elusive, some high and difficult to reach.

One Sunday we were at a favourite haunt, a rainforest on the outskirts of Kandy, and saw a species new to us. We knew from the book that it was called the Plane - a brilliant small purple butterfly with a long curvy tail on its lower wings. The trouble was it was flying about twenty feet high amongst the foliage of the trees. We soon stripped off a branch of a sapling, and using our tee-shirts to bind this to a net, we waited patiently for it to settle on a leaf. When it finally did, Richard cautiously brought the net close to and under the leaf on which it was settled and was just about ready to swoop when it flew away. This happened twice more and we were getting frustrated. Alex said, "Give it to me. Let me have a go."

Just then it settled again and Richard said, "Wait, I've got this," and swung the net up, under the leaf, just in time, over the butterfly and to the right, scooping it into the net, and we all watched as he saw that it was near the bottom of the net and turned it over trapping our first Plane. That, we thought, was our excitement for the day and we were in high spirits.

But a little later we came across a dead green snake about a metre in length lying across the sandy pathway in the forest. We thought we'd have some fun with it, scooped it up and put it in our bag of collector's items, and took it home.

The house we lived in had the bedrooms down one side and the living rooms down the other. The bedrooms were on the left and the sitting rooms on the right. The room occupied by Alex Richard and I had a two-tier bunk bed for Alex and Richard, and a single bed for me. It was the third bedroom down, opposite the dining/breakfast room.

Each morning our cousin Dorothy, who occupied the room next to us, opposite the sitting room, would wake up and go into the breakfast area to put the water on to make our morning cup of tea, We woke before her that morning, and set the snake down on the dining table in a zig-zag arrangement and rushed back into bed.

We heard her as she woke up and made her way into the dining room to put the water on. Next thing we heard her shriek, "Mum! There's a snake in the house!" as she flew back to the front bedroom where her mother was sleeping. We rushed out, retrieved the snake, and put it away with our butterfly equipment and awaited developments.

Our Aunt Gwen and Dorothy came into the dining room as Dorothy was frantically explaining that, "It was moving across the table, getting ready to pounce on me." By this time we had gone out to see what all the fuss was about, and everyone was anxiously looking all over the house for the snake.

The maid, (the little old lady who did our cooking) talked to Aunt Gwen and said she would go out and consult a psychic she knew, to find out more about this. Off she went, to return about an hour later. She sat Aunt Gwen down and explained to her what the psychic had told her. "It's a manifestation of your husband (who had passed away sometime earlier). He has come back with a message for you." She didn't say what the message was, but next thing everyone in the house was looking in every nook and corner for the snake.

I grabbed a flashlight and joined in the search. We went from room to room. I was in Dorothy's room looking under her bed. It was an old house and as I waved the flashlight against the wall I noticed almost at ground level that there was a hole in the wall and I could see two eyes peering out in the beam of the flashlight. I felt the hairs in the nape of my neck rise as I looked into those eyes, getting the fright of my life. In hindsight, I should have said, "Uncle Willie, is that you?" But I just switched off the flashlight and got the hell out of there.

Needless to say, no one ever found the snake, nor did we find out what the message was. And I still don't know what I was looking at in the beam of the flashlight.

Later that morning we showed off our Plane butterfly to Bernard and Robin, and when they asked us where we caught it, we gave them a location at the opposite end of the forest to where we caught it.

We didn't feel bad as we knew they would have done the same. Karma must have got us though because a week later they came home with a Plane.

We made wooden breeding cages with a glass-sided frontage, and brought home caterpillars on their food plants, and watched fascinated, as they grew, moulted, changed into a chrysalis, and then emerged as a butterfly. They would crawl out of their chrysalis skins when fully developed, with their wings curled up over the backs of their thorax, and pump air into their veins till they straightened. Then they would spread their wings, gently waving them up and down till they dried, before flying away in search of nectar to start their life cycle all over again.

Chapter Eleven

Weekends were spent outdoors capturing and studying butterflies. We would pack a lunch and head out after breakfast and come back home in the evening. We climbed all the mountains around Kandy. A by-product of our butterfly catching days was getting an intimate knowledge of weather patterns.

There was a favourite mountain we climbed called Hantane, which was a landmark of Kandy, rising steeply on the western side with a sheer drop on the eastern side, which we viewed as we reached the summit. This was no doubt the manifestation of a crater formed in that location centuries ago. We climbed through villages of estate workers and tea plantations and wound our way past mountain creeks before we reached the grassy steep climb to the summit. On the way down we often stopped by a pool at the base of a little waterfall and had a dip in the cool water before having our picnic lunch. Then it would be time to stretch out on a rock by the stream, fanned by a gentle breeze, and gaze up at the blue sky through the softly swaying foliage of the tree under which we lay, watching white clouds drift away in a blue sky.

Another mountain we climbed in the region was called Hunnasgiriya. The elevation at its peak was 950 metres or 3117 feet, where it was said to be haunted and was reputed to have a ghost that would throw rocks at noon every day at anyone who climbed it.

We had chosen a cloudy day in June and had to climb through the jungle, the path leading over a small bridge beside a rock pool beneath yet another waterfall. The climb took us up the side of the waterfall. It began to drizzle, a fine misty rain. There were five of us on the climb, the two D'Abrera's and us three Gogerly brothers.

The path was steep and slippery and Bernard tripped on a rock. "Shit! I've twisted my ankle!" He leaned against the branch of a tree and pulled his left ankle up with his right hand, bending down to massage it gingerly. We stopped, waiting to see how bad it was. "It's okay, he said after a while. "Just gave me a bit of shock. I'm fine."

We continued, having to pass through a row of tenement houses of Tamil plantation labourers imported from India to work on the extensive tea plantations. A little kid sat on a step in the front of one of the meagre houses with a black cat on his lap, watching us walk by. He must have been about eight and had a mop of unruly hair hanging over his eyes and a big toothy grin on his face as he watched us, stroking the cat. His mother must have been out picking tea with the rest of the crew. A couple of men were in a conversation in a doorway. Outside another house a black and white dog was wagging his tail furiously, trying to get at a rodent of some sort that had scampered between a rock and the step leading to the house. He was barking excitedly and pawing at the ground in frustration.

We walked on, up into a large tea plantation. Between the myriad tea bushes were profuse raspberry plants laden with fruit. We picked handfuls and stuffed them in our shirts as we climbed. Scattered amongst the tea bushes lithe Indian women, carrying large cane baskets on their backs were picking their quota of tea leaves for the day.

The correct way was to pick two leaves and a bud and throw it over their shoulder into the basket. They did this all day until their baskets were full and they would take it to the weighing station, to get their pay for the day. On this day the bushes were lush after the recent heavy rain, and you could tell it was a good crop and it wouldn't take as long as it usually did to fill their baskets. They wore colourful labourer's sarees, robes tucked in at the waist, and slung over their shoulder. They chattered amongst themselves, as they worked, and laughed at some joke they shared. They were demure and shy in the presence of strangers and looked at us inquisitively and smiled if they made eye contact.

Then we entered a forest as we made our way to the crest of the mountain. It was raining steadily now as we picked our way through wet undergrowth, little rivulets forming, across the track as we trudged. Rain slid down through the forest trees and birds settled on branches, as drops of rain dripped off their wings. We reached the summit about noon but the ghost must have had a day off because there were no rocks thrown at us.

A heavy mist lay over the valley below denying us a view of the vista that lay beneath. We were soaked. We ate our picnic lunch by a rock under a tree, and after a while started our descent.

Leeches inhabited the undergrowth and found their way onto us as we passed. Like little worms, they had three sucking lips, with which they would attach themselves to the warmest part of their host and feast on their blood.

Alex found one at the back of his knee and reacted, "Shit, shit, shit I've got a leach!" he yelled.

"Don't pull it off," I said. "You know if you do it will never stop bleeding." This is because leeches secrete an anticoagulant that keeps the blood from clotting and allows the blood to keep flowing until the leech is full. If you pull them off your skin it takes long for the bleeding to stop. And the site may get infected.

"I can't just leave it there," he said, "It's creepy."

"Don't worry," I replied, "I remembered to bring some salt."

Salt was the solution to the problem, as leaches detach themselves if they are doused with salt. I took out the container of salt from my duffle bag and sprinkled some on the leach. We all gathered around and watched as the leech drew itself in, sort of scrunching itself up, before falling to the ground.

On the way down, just by the waterfall, we captured some specimens of what was known as the Tree

Nymph. It was also called the ghost butterfly, a pale blue-grey large beauty with black veins. It had a slow loping flight whence it got its name. This was the only location where this species could be found.

That day the D'Abrera's and Gogerly's climbed together so there was no need to compete. The rain had stopped and it had turned into a hot afternoon. As we walked down further we came across a wide pathway covered by packed white sand. Sleeping across it sunning himself on this lazy afternoon was a long brown snake. It was known to be non-poisonous but we gave it a wide berth as we walked past it.

 We had eaten most of the raspberries we stuffed down our shirts and discarded the rest as we reached the main road and waited for the bus to take us back home.

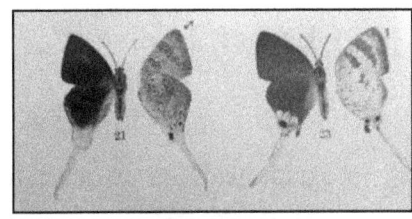

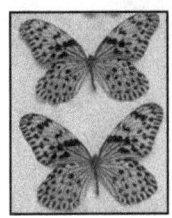

Chapter Twelve

We were a well-known sight in Kandy with our butterfly nets in hand, walking to start a climb or waiting for a bus to take us to our hunting ground for the day. So much so that we became identifiable as butterfly collectors in the town.

One afternoon when there came a knock at the door, and a representative of Horizon Pictures stood there to talk to us, it took us by surprise. Horizon Pictures were shooting that epic movie 'Bridge over the River Kwai' with William Holden, Alex Guinness, and Jack Hawkins, in Sri Lanka.

They had heard that we collected butterflies and wanted to hire some boxes from our collection to use as background material for a scene they were shooting in Kandy.

To say we were excited would be an understatement. First, we were overwhelmed that Horizon Pictures had heard of our butterfly collection. Next, we were thrilled and overcome with surprise that they wanted to hire some of our collection for the movie.

When I answered the knock at the door I didn't know who to expect. Standing there was someone who I recognised as American when he started talking.

"Hi," I said. "Can I help you?"

"Joe Spiteri, Horizon Pictures. Does Robert Gogerly live here?"

(Gulp! He knows my name! Wow!)

"Err, yes," I replied, surprised and excited, "That's me."

"We've heard you guys have a butterfly collection, is that right?"

"Yes, it is," I said. "How can we help?"

"We'd like to hire some of your collection to use in the movie we are shooting here in Kandy - 'Bridge over the River Kwai'. We'll pay you guys for it."

(Wow, wow, wow! And we get paid to hire some of our collection out? To Horizon Pictures? With William Holden, Jack Hawkins, and, and…Alec Guinness? Am I dreaming or what?)

By this time Alex and Richard had come to the door and were kind of struck dumb, listening to what was going down.

"Err … y . . . y …yes," I stammered, "That would be great."

"Please come in," I said. "So rude of me."

"Not at all," he replied. "I can tell this has come as a surprise."

We took him into the sitting room and showed him our collection. He was impressed and said they would provide glass-fronted cases, and we could fill them up.

They were to be hung on the wall of the set of an army Office and used as background material for a scene to be shot with Jack Hawkins discussing battle tactics with an army officer. They were going to pay us what to us school kids was a small fortune.

He said goodbye and left, saying they would send over the glass-fronted cases in a couple of days and pick them up for shooting the next day.

We were ecstatic and couldn't wait to tell our friends. We even became mini-celebrities as part of Horizon Pictures 'associates'!

We went to the location they were shooting, only a couple of miles away in a house on a hill overlooking a sweeping valley below, and watched Jack Hawkins in his war room discussing strategy, with our butterflies hanging on a wall in the background.

Our three minutes of reflected fame.

Chapter Thirteen

In the heart of Kandy, a picturesque artificial lake lies serene and peaceful. It was built in 1807 by Sri Wickrama Rajasinghe the last king of Kandy and the last ruling monarch of Sri Lanka. It took five years to build and a walk around it amongst shady trees is a distance of 3.4 kilometres (about 2 miles). It has an island at the south-central part where it is deepest at 18.5 metres (almost 60 feet). This is the broadest part of the lake which narrows a little to the north.

Legend has it that the small island at its centre was used by the king's harem for bathing and was connected to the palace by a secret tunnel.

Our scoutmaster Anton Blacker persuaded the school Principal to stretch the budget to allow for the purchase of a small sailing boat, which was moored at the boathouse along the southern border. It was for the use of the school Scouts and Rover Scouts. It was named "Louis" in honour of our school's founder.

It was time to learn to sail. We had to learn to tack and jibe, raise and lower the sail, how to handle the boom, and most importantly, stay afloat. When I think about it now I realise what risk I put myself at because I didn't know how to swim, and we never carried life jackets. Come to think of it, I don't think any of us were ever asked if we could swim.

But it was fun. Learning to tack upwind, then jibing to turn around and sail in the opposite direction downwind, was exhilarating and exciting. I remember the time when we were out on the lake in the early days of our learning, when a lull in the wind caused the boat to stall and a sudden gust of wind caused the sail to billow. One of the guys in the boat named Ruparatne, yelled, "Boom bugger coming! Boom bugger coming!" as the boom swung in from the wind. We had to duck under the boom and pull it in to gain control to prevent the boat from keeling over.

The first day we sailed on the "Louis" was a Friday afternoon in May. Four of us Rover Scouts (Ashley. Dempsey, Faisal, and I) boarded a bus outside the school gates, with our scoutmaster Anton Blacker, and alighted at the boathouse on the south side of the lake.

We got our first look at the 'Louis' bobbing up and down in a gentle swell. Her hull was painted white with black trim and LOUIS was painted in black near the bow.

"Okay boys," said Anton. "Hop in and let's get started."

We rowed out into the open water and had our first lesson. After explaining the basics to us, Anton took his position at the helm, in control of the tiller. The boat was facing north from where a steady breeze was blowing on a warm sunny afternoon. The mast was set, the boom attached to it and the single main sail was hoisted, under directions from Anton. Time to move.

Anton changed direction with the tiller pointing the bow into the wind but at an angle and said, "Ready to tack!"

"Ready sir!" I replied and set the sail at a 45-degree angle. The wind from the starboard (right) side of the boat caught the sail and we were away, gliding smoothly through the water at a 45-degree angle, picking up speed as the wind increased. Water sprayed behind us in a spreading white wake, as the boat listed to port and we leaned over to starboard to keep it from capsizing.

As we approached the western perimeter of the lake Anton adjusted the tiller and said, "Prepare to jibe." We replied in unison.

"Ready sir!"

The boat swung around to starboard and as the boom swung around at the turn we ducked beneath it, and I trimmed the sail again to catch the wind from the north, and we sped across the lake towards the east. We zig-zagged our way up the lake till it was time to turn around and sail straight downwind with full sail to get back to the boathouse.

"Watch your head," Ashley yelled, as the boom swung around, and I ducked.

"Thanks," I said, and we were on our way back. Faisal and Dempsey talked excitedly, and we thanked Anton for letting us have this experience.

"Glad you enjoyed it," he said and dashed our hopes of a repeat the next day. "Different crew tomorrow."

I was with my best friend Ashley, in the school library. We had just browsed through some magazines on sailing and walked out together to stand by the waist-high railing on the balcony. Leaning our elbows on the top we watched the students on the lawn below. Kids were wandering around in their school uniforms, - white shirt, and navy blue shorts.

"Hey Ashley," I said. "I wonder what the bottom of the lake looks like. I mean, how flat it is, and does it have ridges and undulations?"

"Never thought about it," he replied, "What made you ask?"

"I was thinking, maybe we could do an underwater map - I think it's called a bathymetric map - of the lake."

"How would we do that? We don't have any equipment."

"I was thinking, what if we drew a map of the lake, got some rope, tied knots along its length, say about a foot apart, tied a brick to the bottom as an anchor, and then hop in the school boat and row around the perimeter. We could drop the rope over the side and count the knots from where the brick lands at the bottom, up to the water level, and mark its depth on the map."

"Keep going, I'm interested."

"We'd have to do this all around the perimeter, marking the depth on the map. Then we would have to do the same at a distance further away from the edge of the lake and row around the inner perimeter, marking the depths at regular intervals. Once we cover the whole lake from outside to the centre, we would have to join the dots with the same depth and we'd have a map showing the shape, or relief, of the lake bed."

"Just the same as contour maps." Ashley commented.

"Yep," I said. "What do you reckon? Want to give it a go?"

"Why not," he said. "It would be interesting. Count me in. When shall we start?"

"How about tomorrow? It's Saturday, and the weather's supposed to be fine."

"Sure," he said. "Dad's got heaps of rope in his shed, and I bet I can find a brick there too. I'll do the rope, with the knots a foot apart, you do the map – you're good at that sort of thing."

"Okay," I replied. "It's a deal."

We went to our respective homes that afternoon to prepare for our project, eager to start.

I drew a map as accurately as I could.

The next morning, as agreed, we met at the boathouse, with our equipment, ready to go. I had picked up the keys from Anton who asked what we were up to, and when I told him he thought it was very enterprising of us, and wished us luck.

Ashley had the long coil of rope. He had tied knots a foot apart, along the length of the rope. At each knot, he had tied a green ribbon. At every fifth knot, it was yellow. We laid out the rope at the edge of the road beside the boathouse to check. We had 52 knots with green ribbons and 12 with yellow ribbons, with a brick firmly attached to where the 13th ribbon would have been. That gave us a plumb line of 65 feet. We coiled up the rope and took it aboard the 'Louis'. I had the map on a clipboard with a pen, and we were ready.

We rowed out to the south-western corner of the lake, near the spillway to begin our project.

"Okay, here we go!" I said at the stern of the boat with the oars. Ashley dropped the plumbline over the edge letting it out until he felt the brick touch the bed of the lake. We were at the edge of the lake, and it wasn't deep. He pulled up the line and counted the knots from the brick to the water level. It was up to the first yellow ribbon.

"Five feet," he said, "pretty shallow." I marked the depth on the map. And rowed north, the same distance away from the perimeter. We stopped and repeated the process.

"It's just over five, - again." he said.

It was getting hot and humid and I could feel the sweat running down the back of my neck.

We continued around the perimeter, sharing rowing and plumbing duties. Then we went in a few feet in from the perimeter, and went around again in ever-decreasing distances, marking the depth on the map till we had covered the entire lake.

Near the island, the plumbline went down, down, down with no sign of the brick hitting the bottom. We were beginning to run out of line and I thought, "Crap! How deep is this part?" Then I felt the brick hit the bottom. The line showed the last yellow ribbon on the rope. "Holy cow! That's sixty feet. Nearly ran out of plumbline." That was the deepest part of the lake.

"Whew, that was hard work," I said as we moored at the boathouse. Ashley wiped the sweat from his brow with a stiff index finger, moving it across his forehead and flicking the sweat away.

"Well, it's over now," Ashley replied. "Let's get some lunch and a drink." After a sandwich and drink at a nearby café, we took a bus back home and laid the map on the desk in my room.

I joined the dots showing the same distance and a picture of the bed of the lake began to appear on the map. Using different coloured pens for areas of increasing depth, I coloured in the map and saw how the depth increased from the edge to the centre, but not evenly. We saw again that the deepest part of the lake was near the island.

This meant that the area had been built up where the island was located so that it would be surrounded by deep water. We figured that the King had ordered that, to make access to the island difficult. That laid to rest the legend of a secret tunnel from the island to the palace.

On Monday we displayed the bathymetric map of the Kandy Lake on the Harrow house wall (news) paper, a broadsheet with articles of interest from students in a locked glass-fronted cabinet. Students gathered around to view what was on display at each house wallpaper and that Monday Harrow house readers had something different to view. It generated a lot of interest.

My friend George was amongst those around the notice board. "Hey Robert," he said. "Nice work by you and Ash."

"Thanks. George."

"Last time you had such a crowd around here was when you responded to LB's comment about the Gogerly boys destroying nature."

I laughed. "Yeah, I remember. I reminded him that if he had the right to say we were destroying nature because we collected butterflies, then I had the right to remind him that he was doing the same each time he sat down to a meal, whether it was meat, fish, or vegetables."

"Good come back, that was."

"That's not all," I said. "Couple of days later Alex, Richard, and I fired some firework rockets from the gaps in the back wall of his property into his courtyard. Pretty juvenile behaviour I know but it made us feel good."

Chapter Fourteen

I was not comfortable in social situations in groups that did not share similar interests to me although it was impossible to evade such situations in class sizes of thirty-five to forty. Or to avoid some bullying. Some boys in my class at the time resented the fact that I was getting good grades, and took their resentment out by bullying me.

I had to walk through a corridor between two classrooms to get to my desk, and after recess, kids would line up on either side of the corridor and wait for me. As I neared the corridor I would hear them whisper. "He's coming, be ready." Then as I started my walk through the corridor they would shove me from one side to the other as I walked.

In the beginning, I would react, "What are you doing? Just leave me alone. I've done nothing to you." They would just snigger and keep up the shoving. I felt too intimidated to fight back – I was outnumbered anyway.

Getting there early was one way to avoid this bullying, so I would rush back after eating my lunch in the cafeteria, or take sandwiches with me and eat them at my desk and read for the rest of the time before classes resumed. I felt dejected and unhappy but had to endure these bullying instances when they occurred. Finally, because I did not react, I expect, they tired of it and left me alone.

There was one boy who made me his favourite victim and constantly bullied me. He made it a point to wait for me when school was out and walk home with me. His home was closer to our school than mine was and as we walked he would pinch me in the shoulder or punch me incessantly. I was too timid to fight back. If I said, "Leslie, just leave me alone, will you? What's the matter with you?" He would reply with something like, "Scaredy cat, scaredy cat, mummy's boy just fancy that – you can't stop me anyway."

One afternoon I'd had enough. Just as we reached his house, before he turned in at the gate he gave me a last punch for the day on the shoulder.

That was when something snapped in me. I saw red, and before I realised what I was doing, I swung my right arm straight from my hip and struck him with a fierce slap on his left cheek. It snapped his head to the side as his cheek turned red.

His eyes opened wide in surprise (I'll never forget the stunned look on his face) and he said, "What'd you do that for?"

I replied, "Just so you'd know what it's like."

He didn't say another word, just walked in the gate.

I walked the rest of the way home feeling strangely elated.

He never touched me again.

One day we were walking home after cricket practice, - Quintus, Sarath, and I.

We had decided to walk on the railway track which ran parallel to the road, behind rows of houses, the rail track, and the road being about one hundred yards apart.

"Herbert's batting is improving," said Quintus.

I replied, "But I bowled him round his legs with my googly!"

"Good one," Sarath said, and then, "hey! There's that guy selling fabrics."

Walking about 30 feet ahead of us was a burly middle-aged Afghan vendor of fabrics. He had a bundle on his head which contained his stock of fabrics which he was selling. He'd walk the streets holding the bundle aloft and announce at regular intervals.

"Rethee – up! Rethee - up!" (Which meant 'Fabrics for sale, fabrics for sale'). He had made his last sale for the day and was walking home.

Quintus brought his fingers to his lips indicating to us to be quiet, walked up behind him on the railway sleepers, and tipped the bundle over from on top of his head. The three of us raced away from the scene, accompanied by frighteningly threatening words and loud curses as he bent over to retrieve his bundle. We ran away from the railway tracks to the road and continued on our way home, laughing about what we had done.

About ten minutes later we approached a strip of shops on our right. At the end of the strip was a lane and at the top of the lane just behind a bakery was the Afghan fabric vendor. He was waiting for us.

He spotted us at the same moment we saw him and he charged at us bellowing, "Come here, you thugs! Let me teach you a lesson."

We raced off in three different directions, scared out of our wits. Quintus headed back the way we had come, Sarath raced ahead, and I took off down Primrose Street on the opposite side of the road. The burly middle-aged Afghan was no match for three spritely teenagers, and we were sure we would outrun him.

We caught up with each other about fifteen minutes later at my home.

"Did you see which way he went?" Sarath asked.

"No, I raced up Primrose Street," I replied.

Quintus said, "I saw him coming after me, but I outran him and he gave up."

That was our entertainment for the evening.

Chapter Fifteen

I had started to take an interest in girls. Suddenly they were not just sisters of friends. I began to take real notice of them. I felt an attraction that I hadn't felt before. I liked the way they looked, their long dark hair, their sparkling eyes, the shape of their face, and curves in places we boys would never have. I felt stirrings that I hadn't noticed before.

But I was shy. Shy and nervous in their presence, and lacking in confidence.

I had my first crush on a schoolteacher. She taught children in the Primary School. I first noticed her in the schoolyard one cloudy day when she was walking towards me. She was tall with long wavy dark hair beautiful hazel eyes and an oval face. Those attractive curves were covered by a red saree woven around her and slung over her shoulder. But I was aware of them as they pushed out against the white sleeveless top she was wearing. She had a graceful sinuous walk that caused a stirring in me that was a new experience. I noticed that she was looking straight at me as we crossed. We made eye contact and my heart lurched in my chest. These were feelings I had not felt before and I was confused, but also excited. Her name was Indranee.

Most of my friends and other students at Kingswood lived along the main road between Colombo and Kandy in the section that was known as Peradeniya Road, or on streets just off it. Girls High School was less than a mile away from Kingswood so there were a lot of friends of both schools and sexes around.

The next time I noticed Indranee was a few days later when she was walking home after school. I was home already and had come to the front door as she walked by. We made eye contact again and she smiled at me. I smiled back at her and then she was gone. I learned that she lived at a place called Piachaud Gardens about a quarter of a mile away.

I found I was thinking about her a lot and would rush home every day and stand at my front door just to see her walk by, and see her smile. That was all there was to it and after a while, I grew out of it.

Times were different then and parents were very protective of their daughters. Parents often discouraged friendship with boys in their teens. A common and accepted mode of communication between boys and girls with a crush on each other was by the passing of notes between them. Either surreptitiously as they passed on the street, or through friends. It must be remembered that most people didn't have phones at that time. If you wanted to make a call you would have to go to the Post Office. If it was long-distance you would have to book it at the Post Office and would be told what time to come back to make the call, usually hours later.

One day Dennis, who was a classmate, said to me, "Hey Robert, I hear that there's a girl named Maureen at Girls High School who is interested in you."

"Oh yeah?" I replied, "And how do you know this?"

"Christine told me," he said. Christine was his girlfriend who lived up the street. "She wants to write to you," he continued, "and wants to know if you would like to hear from her."

"Sure," I replied, "Why not?" He just smiled at me and I forgot this conversation as days went by.

After a few days, Dennis came up to me and handed me a note. "This is from Maureen," he said. "She gave it to Christine to give me."

I unfolded the note when I got home and read it.

"Dear Robert,

You don't know me, but I saw you when you visited your mother at the cafeteria last week.

I was immediately attracted to your beautiful green eyes and your good looks. Oh! Handsome! Is it from the Gods you have descended? I would love to meet you and get to know you. Please reply through Christine and let me know if you care to meet me.

Anxiously awaiting your reply,

Maureen."

Hmmm, I thought, is this for real? I had no idea who Maureen was, but I was curious.

And very naïve.

So I replied through Dennis and Christine, thanking her for the letter and saying it would be great if we could meet. We exchanged a few letters, and she said she had to be careful about where we met because her parents hardly ever let her out of the house. The letters became more and more flowery and I was getting more and more impatient to meet her.

Then one day, I was talking to my friend Sarath, and he said to me, "You know you will never meet Maureen, Robert." I thought back to the time Dennis first told me about her, and I remembered the smile on his face when I said, "Why not?" When he asked me if I would accept that first note from her.

It was then the realisation hit me that I had been set up. There was no Maureen. Someone was writing those notes playing on my gullibility and vulnerability. This was all entertainment for them.

I said to Sarath, "You think I'm stupid? I knew all along that you guys had set me up. I'm having fun!"

I decided to play along with them and made my letters passionate and full of flowery phrases. After all, this was what they wanted, and I gave it to them in spades. I said how anxious I was to meet her and that I dreamt about her every night, and couldn't wait to hold her in my arms and kiss her passionately on her luscious lips.

They must have eventually realised that I was on to them, or maybe Sarath said something to them, and the letters suddenly stopped. Nothing was said by anybody, and I didn't call them out on their scheme.

I just put it down to experience.

Chapter Sixteen

It was 1956 and I had just turned eighteen.

"Kingswood Week" was the first weekend in June. It was an occasion when we celebrated and reviewed the past year. Past pupils would come down for the week and would join students, family, friends, and staff in the activities.

Preparations went on all week and the first event was the Inter-House Sports Meet on Friday afternoon. Students were vying for the Crowther Shield for sporting achievement.

Athletes were in their running shorts and white sleeveless tops with numbers stencilled on, in colours, red for Rugby, blue for Winchester, yellow for Eton, and maroon for Harrow. They were milling around, talking animatedly, waiting to be called for their event.

Students and visitors watched from the embankment by the side of the track cheering for their favourites. Announcements over the public address system called for competitors to take their place at the start of the 100 yards final. I had barely won my semi-final heat and had made the final.

I was in the second lane and took my place on the starting blocks, crouched down, leaning back and then forward on my heels, to release the tension in my legs. My heart was racing with nervous anticipation. I stood up with the other runners flicking my wrists to loosen them, hopping from one foot to the other with nervous energy eager to be released.

The starter took up his position alongside the runners and raised the starting pistol.

"Get on your marks!" he barked.

We settled onto the blocks in a starting crouch, extending our fingers onto the track, as we adjusted our positions, at the ready.

"Get set!" he roared, and Nimal broke the line as he started too soon. Two warning shots from the starting pistol indicated a false start as we stumbled forward with Nimal's advance. We only had one warning.

We settled once again, our rhythm interrupted. We had no time to dwell on this. The starter said, 'SET,' a second before we heard the starting gun, and we were off!

I was off to a good start, pushing off the blocks the instant the gun went off, and streaked down the tightly packed sandy track, taking an early lead. I could hear the six other finalists pounding down the track, but held my lead in the few seconds it took to reach the finishing line, only to be pipped on the post at the very last second by Gamini, our House Athletics Captain, who thrust out his chest to breast the tape a whisker ahead of me.

We tailed off past the finishing line as the officials recorded our finishing positions and times.

I went up to Gamini and put my arms around his shoulder.

"Well done," I said.

"You made it hard for me," he replied. "At least we got the major points for the Shield."

The spectators cheered and I heard someone yell, "Well done Harrow! Great run, Gamini."

Someone else called out, "Bad luck Robert. Good run anyway."

The afternoon was full of excitement as the competition for the Crowther Shield hotted up.

Harrow featured prominently on the track, while Rugby took the honours in the field events, Herbert breaking a record in the Triple Jump.

Towards the end of the afternoon Rugby and Harrow were just a few points away from the Shield.

The visitors' race, a short sprint, was won by a girl named Jeanne. More about her later.

It was down to the last race to decide who would take the Shield. Rugby was on 62 points and Harrow 61. The Mile Race was the last for the day and the traditional end to the Meet. There were three points for the winner and two points for the Runner-Up. Harrow needed to win to take the Shield. The problem was Rugby's runner, Nimal, was the favourite.

An outsider, Roy, took an early lead, while Nimal, and Harrow's Ronald settled in, in the main bunch.

The lead changed several times, and as the bell for the last lap sounded Nimal led by six feet, with Ronald hard on his heels. The spectators were urging the runners on. "Come on Rugby."

"Keep it up Nimal!"

"Go, Ronald, you can do it!"

"Come on Harrow. COME ONNNN HARROW!"

They rounded the final bend and entered the straight. The gap was closing.

"Come On Rugby, KEEP IT UP, NIMAL!"

"COME ON, HARROW!"

Fifty yards to go. Nimal was in front by four feet.

Ronald pushed himself to keep up with him.

Twenty-five yards. Nimal was still in front straining nerve and sinew to keep the lead. Ronald pushed on, legs pumping rhythmically, straining every muscle. Two feet behind now.

Nimal stole a glance over his shoulder, he could feel Ronald breathing down his neck

"Go, Ronald, GO, GO, GO!"

"Come ON Rugby."

Fifteen yards to the finish! They were neck and neck! The spectators were frantic.

Ten yards – Nimal.

Five yards - Ronald straining every muscle in his legs. Pushing his chest forward.

With one last surge, he breasted the tape inches ahead of Nimal.

He'd done it! Harrow had won!

The Shield was theirs!

The runners flopped down on the track, nodding to each other, exhausted.

The spectators applauded, the Rugby supporters magnanimous in defeat. They appreciated a good race and graciously acknowledged the winner.

This is how it should be.

We hurried home for a quick early dinner, then it was back to school for the Kingswood Week Concert. A feature of the concert was two short plays presented by the winners of the Inter-House Drama Competition completed a few weeks earlier. Harrow had won that Competition and their play was the main feature of the night, the last item in the concert.

The first play was 'What Men Live By' by Rugby (again). My brother Alex played in it. It was a dramatic adaptation from Tolstoy's 'Michael'.

Next came the main event, 'The Poetasters of Ispahan' by Harrow.

I was in the leading role of Hallaj, a Persian letter-writer, the only scribe in ancient Ispahan.

The curtain rose after intermission and I was on stage in red Persian robes, a yellow shirt, black vest, and a white turban. I said my opening lines –

"Well met, my friends, and be of good cheer,

For never since Allah created man

Was life more goodly to live

Than here in the City of Ispahan!"

We were on the way.

The Plot.

Ibn Hassim a leading businessman had offered his beautiful daughter's hand in marriage to whoever entered a competition, by the payment of five gold coins, and composed the best poem in her honour.

As Hallaj was the only one in town who could present a scroll to Ibn Hassim with the poem, would-be suitors came to him for help. The butcher, the baker, the town tailor, and the barber visited Hallaj with the poems they had composed. Hallaj wrote them down as they dictated.

Then, eager to win by any means, they all came back, one at a time, and requested Hallaj to alter their opponent's poems, to each of their advantages. Cunning Hallaj, who was short of gold coins himself, so he could enter, agreed to do so for the payment of a gold coin.

He made the necessary changes and when Ibn Hassim and his daughter Silvermoon, met at the appointed time and place to hear the poems, he read them out to Ibn Hassim and Silvermoon.

He had by now composed his poem. The poems were reviewed by Ibn Hassim, none of them complimentary to Silvermoon, except Hallaj's which extolled her beauty with promises to love and protect her for the rest of her life.

Needless to say, there were four angry men ready to wreak vengeance on Hallaj, but Ibn Hassim declared Hallaj the winner, and he won his girl.

The next morning Shirl Lisk, a friend of my uncle and ex-student of Kingswood, visited us at home, with his daughter Jeanne.

Jeanne had won the Visitor's Race at the Sports Meet the previous day and I told her "Well done." She was a little older than I, had pretty brown eyes, beautiful cupids bow lips, and an attractive oval face.

She looked at me with an expression that seemed to indicate attraction, and I was flattered.

We talked about the events of the previous day.

"I loved you as Hallaj," she said. "You looked so good in that Persian gear with the turban and everything, and those green eyes! Wow! Roger, I'm glad Dad brought me over on this visit."

We talked some more and I felt myself being drawn to her. There was a definite connection happening between us. I could tell she had been attracted to my character 'Hallaj'.

They stayed for lunch and we got to know more about each other. She had a brother, John, and she had just finished her school career at a Girls' school in Colombo. Her father was a Post Master at a large Post Office in Colombo, seventy-two miles away on the coast.

I found myself wishing they'd stayed longer when their visit ended.

In the evening Kingswood Week continued with the Prize Giving in the school hall.

An Englishman Mr. B. H. Farmer, a popular public figure, was Chief Guest and Mrs. Farmer gave away the prizes. Prizes were distributed for academic achievement and Special Prizes for winners of Competitions in Singing, Oratory, Elocution, Essay Writing, and English Literature.

The most coveted prize of the occasion was the Donhorst Prize for English Literature presented by a generous school benefactor. To win, contestants had to read two prescribed literary books and attend an examination. That year there were only two contestants, Andrew who was a senior student, and I. The prescribed books that year were Shakespeare's 'Macbeth,' and Robert Browning's 'Pippa Passes.'

I had left my reading to the last minute and it was a scramble to finish in time for the Examination, so I wasn't very confident. Exam Day came around and Andrew joined me in the Geography Room that afternoon, where we were handed the examination papers. A while after we started our English Literature master exited the room and left it to us.

I was doing my best to answer the questions and was surprised when I looked Andrew's way to see him peeping under the desktop at the books he had smuggled in. He was referring to them as he framed his answers and I bade goodbye to any hopes of winning.

I never called him out on it and just knew that he had won. Ah! Well, I hoped he was happy. I was apprehensive when, about a week later, the Principal summoned me to his office, and I wondered what I had done wrong.

He extended a hand when I entered his office.

"Congratulations son," he said, "I'm happy to say that you have won the Donhorst Prize for English Literature. You know this prize is not awarded every year unless a certain standard is reached, and you've reached that standard this year. Well done!"

I was surprised and overwhelmed.

They say cheats never prosper.

It was the last prize distributed that evening and I felt a special glow as I accepted it to appreciative applause.

Sunday was the culmination of the festivities with a Church Service in the morning.

There was a dinner that evening for staff and ex-students and I knew Jeanne and her father would be there. I managed to score a ticket from Uncle Willie who had decided not to attend and found myself sitting next to Jeanne at the dinner. Current students were not expected to attend this dinner and I attracted some antagonistic glances, but I didn't care. I wanted to be there. We talked about the weekend and said we'd miss each other when they left. Our arms lightly brushed against each other as we talked and sent little electric currents through my body. I guessed it must have done the same for Jeanne by the way a little shudder seemed to go through her.

"I've had a great time Roger, I'm going to miss you."

"Me too," I replied, "I mean I'll miss you too."

"We can write to each other. Please don't forget me."

"Not a chance," I said, and then the weekend was over.

They left for Colombo the next day and I wrote her a letter telling her how much I enjoyed her company and I said I hoped to hear from her soon.

Days went by and I didn't get the reply I hoped for.

Days turned into weeks. I thought a lot about her and was feeling down.

Then after about six weeks, I received her letter.

Dear Roger,

I found your letter when I came back home! I have been away at my Aunt's place for the last few weeks, but if I had known your letter was here I'd have rushed home like a rocket. It was great to hear from you. I've missed you so much. Please write often.

Love,

Jeanne (Silvermoon).

Our letters got more and more frequent and when I went to Colombo for a weekend I spent the Saturday with her, holding hands and walking in the nearby park, two lovelorn youngsters with stars in their eyes. By now our letters were full of our love for each other and promises to kiss and hold each other when we met. Which we did.

But I was still in school and she had finished her school days and we didn't know where this was going. We wrote to each other every day and I would stand by the front door for the postman on Saturdays waiting anxiously for her letter. I would grab the letter from the postman. Sometimes she would write on the envelope "Run postman run!" and when I replied I would write on the envelope "Hurry! Hurry! Hurry! Get this letter to my honey!" Crazy I know!

I received 99 letters from her. I know because I numbered them all. I never received the 100th.

Suddenly the letters stopped. I waited and waited, but the 'postman went by, - no letter today,' like the Elvis song. I wrote to her asking what was wrong. Had I done something to offend her? Was she ill? What was preventing her from writing? Still nothing.

I felt sad and let down. I had the blues. But time went on and time heals, I stopped thinking about her so often. I stopped dreaming about her. Months went by and she faded to a pleasant memory. Life goes on, no matter what.

I found another love, and that's another story. Years later I received a letter from her saying how sorry she was. She said she hadn't written because she didn't want to hurt me. I was still in school and she had to move on. She was older than I and I guess I couldn't expect her to wait for goodness knows how long for her Hallaj. She had found another.

I visited her a couple of times when I was in Colombo and said I had no hard feelings. We hugged and said goodbye.

Years later when I had started work in Colombo I received an invitation to her wedding.

I thanked her for it but said I couldn't make it. I still cared for her and couldn't see myself 'throwing rice at the girl that I love, just after she said I do,' as the song goes.

Such is love.

Such is life!

As Alfred Lord Tennyson famously said, "It is better to have loved and lost than never to have loved at all."

Hallaj

Chapter Seventeen

It was the cricket season, and Kingswood was playing Trinity – a prestigious College in Kandy. Trinity had a strong team and we were not expected to win. We would have to play above ourselves if we were to make a game of it.

Things did not go well for us and towards the end of the day, we were in a losing position.

We were chasing 242 runs for victory and were 7 down for 147. They needed 3 wickets for victory. Our only hope at avoiding defeat was to hold out for a draw. If we didn't lose all our wickets by the end of the game, we would foil their victory plans and draw the game. This was better than losing.

I was at the batting crease and defending stubbornly. At 152 we lost our eighth wicket and at 157 our ninth. We were staring at defeat when Sarath joined me at the wicket. We were still together at the tea break on 170 for nine wickets. Maurice, our captain encouraged us to keep going.

"Hang in there guys," he said. "We can still draw the game."

My friend Derrick came up to me and said, "Robert, you are batting well, just keep it up. Remember, watch the ball right on to the bat. All you have to do is block it out to the end and we'll be home and hosed."

Yeah, right! I thought, easier said than done.

But we hung in there grimly, not taking any risks, and the end was in sight.

The score crept up slowly, but that wasn't critical. Time was. At 185 for nine I was at the bowler's end and watched as Sarath swung at a ball outside the off-stump and the Trinitians went up in a loud appeal as the ball thudded into the wicket-keeper's gloves and he raised a hand in anticipation, "HOW'S THAT?" they yelled in unison.

I looked back at the umpire in dread. He considered the appeal for a second and then shook his head. "Not out!" Sarath hadn't got a nick as the ball passed his bat. Whew! That was close.

Ten minutes to go.

Then five.

191 for nine. I was at the batsmen's end.

A leg-spinner was bowling. I hated facing leg-spinners.

The first ball pitched on off stump and I let it go through to the wicket-keeper. I knew the ploy was to make me play at it and get a nick as it broke to the off, and be caught behind.

The second ball was dead straight on the middle stump, pitched up, and I put my foot to the pitch of the ball and defended it with a dead bat.

Four to go.

The third ball pitched well outside off stump and I went back to cut it through point as it broke to the off.

Only it broke the other way, missed my pads, and rattled the stumps. I hadn't picked his googly, the one that turned in the opposite direction to a normal leg-break.

All out!

We had lost the game, and Sarath and I walked dejectedly back to the pavilion.

I was expecting a roasting from my team-mates, when all I got was "Bad luck, Robert."

Somehow that made me feel worse than if they had criticized me.

I felt I had let the team down, but then, that's cricket. It's only a game after all.

Our next game was 'away' and we had to travel down to Galle on the south-western coast of the island. We went by train and had to change trains in Colombo.

It was my first 'away' game, but when the team sheet was done, my name wasn't on it and I was the first reserve. We were playing Richmond College on an oval by the sea.

It was my first year, and my first game away, and I knew all 'freshers' had to go through a rite of passage and be initiated into the team. I had heard stories of what this entailed and it was not my cup of tea! Just before hitting our bunks for the night, we would be expected to gather in the common room and strip naked in front of the team and expected to 'perform'.

Then the captain would stand naked on a desk and we would have to stand before him, extend our hand up to touch him, and say, "I am now a fully-fledged member of the Kingswood cricket team."

No way Jose!

I wimped out. My cousin Francis was a doctor in Galle, and I visited him after the game.

At dinner, I asked him, "Francis can I stay over tonight?"

"Sure," he said, "you're most welcome to stay."

His wife Kathleen made up the spare room for me, and after a cup of hot chocolate, I said goodnight and got into bed with a sigh of relief.

I had evaded the initiation ceremony!

When I returned to Richmond College the next morning I expected a roasting from the guys and was surprised when no one said anything to me about the previous night.

Chapter Eighteen

Uncle Ric was posted to Bandarawela, a town in the central mountains, where we spent our Christmas holidays with him in 1956. He had bought a beautiful property on the outskirts of the town, on the side of a mountain, and it wasn't long before he had built a swimming pool and tennis court. His gardens were extensive, full of colour, and well maintained as usual. On this occasion, he resided at his Government supplied townhouse not far from the hospital.

I have a lot to thank Uncle Ric for. Besides paying for my education he was very generous to his extended family, always supporting them and even taking them in when necessary. He was well known and respected as a doctor, and readily made house calls at all hours of the night, for which he did not require payment.

One night after dinner, I was in the sitting room reading "War and Peace". The night was cool and a gentle breeze came in through the open window fanning the blue curtains draped around their frame. Uncle Ric was in the music room next door, on the piano, and the strains of Mozart wafted through the air. As I turned a page, I heard a knock on the front door. I put 'War and Peace' down on the little table by the sofa, and walked to the front door to see who was calling at this hour.

Standing in the portico was a guy, bare-chested and in a sarong, holding his left arm up at the elbow with his right hand. There was a long gash in his forearm almost from wrist to elbow with the skin split open and he was bleeding profusely. He was breathing heavily and in obvious distress. Before I could say anything he said, frantically, "Is the doctor at home?"

"Oh, My God!" I said, looking around for something to staunch the bleeding, "I'll get him." But by now Uncle Ric was at the door.

He took one look and summoned a servant "Edwin!" he yelled, "Fetch some towels, quick." He sat the desperate guy down on the closest chair, as Edwin hurried in with towels, which he carefully wrapped around the wound. Without any fuss he said, "Come with me, let's get you into the clinic so we can fix this up." They walked to the garage, and Uncle Ric drove him down to the hospital, which was five minutes away, for surgery on the gaping wound.

Uncle Ric had many good qualities, but he was a sore loser. He was a good tennis player and won many Club Tennis Championships.

The Bandarawela Tennis Club was holding its annual Tennis Tournament. Uncle Ric was a prominent member of the club and had an outstanding record on the tennis court. He was the defending champion as the previous year's winner.

We all went down to watch the Final, Barbara, Alex, Richard, and I. Uncle Ric had a friend Stanley, living with him at the time, and we formed a little support group.

He had breezed through the early rounds losing just three sets his way to the Final. His opponent was a young up and comer from the nearby Badulla Tennis Club. Ranjan was a brash young teenager, at nineteen, and had no doubts about beating a veteran. At forty-three Uncle Ric may have been past his best, but he had a wealth of experience and a crafty strategic game carefully honed over the years, to his advantage.

He took the first set through deft placement and guile, as opposed to a powerful serve and an erratic game from the youngster. The score was 6-4, with just one break of serve.

Ranjan broke Ric's serve early in the second set and took an early lead. Ric tightened up his game and held serve, but seemed rattled as Ranjan powered down two aces in the next game, and maintained his lead to take the set 6-3.

Final set. All or nothing for both players.

We watched, entranced, from the sidelines with spectators shouting encouragement to both players. Ranjan had brought a contingent of supporters with him that outnumbered the Bandarawela Tennis Club's support for Ric.

"Come on Ric, you can do this." the Club President yelled.

"Go Ranjan!" came the response, "he's past his best. Your turn this year!"

"Rattle him with your serve, Ranjan, move the old man around the court, he's tiring!"

"Play at your own pace Ric, you've got the game to do it. You've got this, Champ!"

Ric served to Ranjan's back-hand. Ranjan returned serve, cross-court. Ric returned down the line just clipping the tramline.

"Out!" called the linesman and Ric gritted his teeth and shook his head. It was a wrong call and he was on the wrong side of it. 0 – 15.

The first four games see-sawed as each player sought an advantage, but at 3-3 it was still anyone's championship.

Then Ranjan unleashed three powerful aces to move ahead, breaking Ric's serve to go 4-3 up and consolidated the break to take the next game to love, and it was 5-3 in Ranjan's favour.

Crunch time.

Ric called on all his reserves, and with accurately placed passing shots clawed back to 5-4, still behind but gaining in confidence. Too eager to reach the finishing line Ranjan double-faulted attempting to dominate with his serve, and Ric broke his serve to level at 5-5.

Ric served again with an ace that lacked Ranjan's power, but it was still an ace. Points went by in a blur and the match went to 6-5 in Ric's favour.

Ranjan was now serving to stay in the match, but Ric was on a roll. With pinpoint accuracy, a cross-court winner kissed the line, and Ranjan was down 30-40, Match Point to Ric.

Ranjan served.

Ace!

The score was 40-40. Deuce. Match point saved.

Ranjan served again, but nerves got the better of him and he found himself facing loss when Ric had another match point.

Again he fought back to deuce (40-40) and served to Ric's body, forcing an awkward return into the net.

Advantage Ranjan. He made no mistake with his next serve and levelled to 6-6.

It was then that age took its toll and a tiring Ric faded away in the next two games to give Ranjan victory and the Championship with a 4-6, 6-3, 8-6 victory.

It was so close and yet so far.

After the presentation, a surly Uncle Ric came out of the clubrooms feeling rattled and irritable.

"No support when I needed it," he muttered. "Where's Stanley?"

Stanley had driven away in Uncle Ric's car while the match was in progress and had not yet returned.

"He's not back yet," I replied. "He took the car and drove off about half an hour ago."

That set him off.

"What?" he asked. "He knew I was in the Final and needed all the support I could get! That young punk had everyone rooting for him. Where was Stanley when I needed him? Where the hell has he gone?"

We all remained silent. It was not a good time to say anything.

He paced about for ten minutes, red-faced and furious. Then he picked up his gear and said, "I guess we'll have to walk home. I'm not hanging around here to watch everyone feeling sorry for me."

It was a fifteen-minute walk home and the conversation was all about his loss.

"Did you see that? I had match-point twice. *Twice,* would you believe, and I could have done with more support. Did you cheer for me?"

"Of course Uncle Ric. Of course, we cheered for you."

"Well, it didn't do any good, did it? I still lost."

There was no answer to that.

"And where the hell is Stanley?" He roared. "That boy's got it coming to him when he gets back!"

We were well aware of that.

He was sweating as we walked. He took a handkerchief (yes we still used those) out of his pocket and mopped his brow. We reached his home and walked slowly down the sloping drive.

Still no sign of Stanley.

A few minutes later we sat down to dinner at a garden setting outside a spreading tree. The servants had hung lanterns on the branches of the trees. It was a picturesque setting. We could smell the pine, as cicadas filled the air with their shrill relentless whine. Glow-worms dotted the air with yellow light. There were four of us. Barbara, Alex, Richard, and I.

We sat at two tables, waiting for Uncle Ric. He joined us in a while, looking a bit more relaxed, and we guessed he had calmed down. He wore a light blue cotton shirt and black shorts. We sipped orange juice from tall glasses as we talked, and dinner was brought to the table.

There was roast beef, potatoes, green beans, and carrots, in a tasty gravy. We were hungry teenagers and we soon tucked in.

"This tastes nice," Barbara said. "The cook has outdone himself today."

Just then we heard the car at the top of the drive, the tyres slowly crunching their way down the gravel.

Uh! Oh! We thought, here comes trouble.

Stanley stopped on the drive just level with us, and he slowly got out of the car.

"I'm sorry, Uncle Ric," he said, but that was as far as he got.

Uncle Ric leaped out of his chair and made straight for Stanley.

"Where the hell have you been?" he roared. "You know what I expect of you. You had no business taking the car, and you knew I expected your support at the club.

And you weren't there when I was ready to come home."

With that, he attempted to strike Stanley who raced down the drive with Uncle Ric in hot pursuit. The last we saw of them was Stanley rounding the far end of the front of the house with Uncle Ric airborne as he aimed a kick at Stanley's back.

We sat in stunned silence for a few minutes before one of the servants, Edwin, came out and said, "Uncle Ric wants you to finish your dinner. He won't be out tonight. We've given him some medication and put him to bed."

We were not aware that he had a medical condition, but I guess it explained what went down that night.

The next morning when we met for breakfast, it was as if nothing had happened the night before.

Not a word was spoken about it then, or at any time after.

We always knew Uncle Ric had a short temper and we tried our best not to annoy him. The worst we had seen up to then, were bouts of irritation when he would snap at servants or us. On one occasion when the soup was served up at the dinner table, he was not happy with it. He called for the cook who came up nervously, to the table.

"What is this?" He asked. "This is not soup. It's pure dishwater!" So saying, he stood up and poured the bowl of soup over the cook's head.

The cook's only response was, "Sorry, sir!"

We felt that if he kept this up there would be retaliation, and it would not be pleasant.

This was probably relative to whatever medical condition was ailing him at the time.

Chapter Nineteen

I was still uncomfortable in social situations where I didn't know anyone. I was with Uncle Ric at the New Year's Eve Dance at the Tennis Club that year. He wanted me to join in the dancing, though I hardly knew any dance steps. I was not confident and didn't want to do it, but Uncle Ric had said, "Go on Roger, just get up there and have fun!" But I didn't want to be there.

The floor was crowded with people from different walks of life. The men wore suits and the women colourful and elegant dresses. The Band struck up 'White Christmas' to introduce the night, as the guests chatted amicably, picking short eats and glasses of wine from a table set up at one end of the hall.

The music changed to something I did not recognize and it was time to dance.

This was the part I dreaded.

I found myself in the outer circle of what was called the 'Paul Jones'. There was an outer circle of guys and an inner circle of girls, and we walked in opposite directions till the music stopped. Then we would dance with whoever was facing us.

The person opposite me was a lady older than I, with dark wavy hair, a kind face, and she wore a bright blue dress flaring to below her knees. She had dark eyes which I noticed as she smiled and moved towards me putting her arms around my waist and on my shoulder, and I did the same to her. I felt awkward and said, "I'm sorry I shouldn't even be here. I don't know how to dance properly."

"That's okay," she replied. "I can see you're nervous. It'll be fine. Just relax and try to follow my steps. I'll help you, don't worry."

The music started again. Thank goodness it was a slow number. I tried to follow her steps as she stepped back and across with her right foot, and I followed with my left. Her movements formed a square, and after a couple of stumbles I got the hang of it and moved to the slow beat of "Smoke Gets in Your Eyes".

"See?" she said, "It's not so bad. You're doing well. Just relax and keep it up." I let my breath out and tried to relax. She was sensitive, and I thought – this is not so bad after all. She started to move me around the floor, and I felt a little more confident.

"What's your name?" she asked.

I replied, "Roger, what's yours?"

"Stacey. You seem like a nice guy. Just do what you're doing and enjoy the night."

"Thank you for helping me," I said. "I don't know what I would have done if it was anyone else. I was hoping a hole would open up in the floor and swallow me up when the music stopped."

"Nonsense," she said. "Look at you now! Just keep it up. You'll be fine." She flicked some stray strands of hair off her face, and I noticed her wedding ring.

Just then the music stopped and we had to change partners. I found myself facing a bright-eyed girl about my age with a mop of dark curls and brown eyes in an eye-catching green dress that clung to her body showing off her curves to advantage.

"Hi," she said cheerily, "I guess it's us then," and moved into my arms.

I replied, "Hi there! Nice to meet you. I hope I don't step on your toes."

"Don't you worry, I don't bite! Well, not hard anyway!" And the ice was broken.

"Roger," I said, and raised my eyebrows questioningly. "Penny," she replied, as I put my right arm around her waist and my left hand on her shoulder. She did the same to me. We moved to the music and I began to enjoy myself. Penny moved sinuously in my arms and I gained confidence as the dance wore on.

"Thanks for the dance," I said when the music stopped.

"You're most welcome. I enjoyed it."

Stacey caught my eye sometime later, and I walked over to her. "How's it going?" she asked.

I replied, "Fine. I'm starting to enjoy myself, thanks to you."

"Glad I could help."

"Can I get you a drink? Wine?"

"Just what I was thinking. White will be fine." And I returned with two glasses of Chablis.

"This is a nice drop," she said, and I agreed with her.

This wasn't so bad after all. Thank you, Uncle Ric.

I scored another dance with Penny later, and we flirted mildly as the night wore on. Penny was fun to talk to, and we were enjoying each other's company. I was drawn to her outgoing nature and her love of life. Her father was a lawyer and her mother a schoolteacher. They were visiting her Aunt for Christmas, whose husband was a member of the tennis club, hence their presence there that night.

She had heard of my Uncle Ric and his loss at the tennis final. Her aunt and uncle were friends and they swapped visits occasionally.

Penny said she would be returning to Colombo in a couple of days, and we said we would write to each other.

"I'm glad we met," she said. "I have enjoyed your company. It's been fun."

"For me too. You're easy to talk to, I was so nervous when my Uncle virtually insisted that I come tonight. I'm usually very shy."

"Not tonight, you weren't."

"That's because you made me feel relaxed in your company. Thank you for that."

"You're welcome."

Midnight came, and we joined hands in a circle to Auld Lang Syne. We wished each other "Happy New Year" with a kiss on the cheek. The noise of whistles and crackers popping filled the air as everyone wished each other and excited chatter continued, till everyone gradually filtered out of the hall and made their way home.

The night had turned out better than I had expected after my initial discomfort and lack of confidence. Thanks again, Uncle Ric.

Chapter Twenty

I belonged to the local Youth Group headed by Anton Blacker and took part in several of their activities including excursions around Kandy.

Penny and I wrote to each other occasionally, but being so far apart it gradually petered out.

One evening at a sing-along at a meeting of the Group at the Kandy Methodist Church Hall a girl in the row ahead of me dropped her handkerchief on the floor and it came to rest near her chair. I picked it up and handed it to her saying, "I think this is yours."

"Thank you," she replied as she took it.

I learned that her name was Jill. She was in her final year at Girls' High School. There were several girls from that school and Kingswood, in the group. We became good friends and as time went on we became more than just friends, spending a lot of time with the group.

I learned that Jill's father had left her mother before she was born. Her mother, Iris, had re-married after a few years, to a Muslim, and she had a half- brother, Jack.

Jack and Jill.

Iris' husband, Ibrahim, was a Muslim, and Muslims are permitted to have seven wives. When he suggested to Iris that he bring home another wife she looked at him with eyes that could kill, and said, "The day you do that is the day I will cut off your penis and feed it to the hyenas."

That was the only time he considered polygamy.

I completed my school career at the end of 1957 and hoping to be a journalist, contacted the "Times of Ceylon," looking for employment. Getting into Journalism was not easy, and it was not what you knew but who you knew that worked for you. They referred me to their sports correspondent in Kandy, a guy named Ben Van Reyk.

I visited him at his home, from where he worked. I tapped at his door and when he opened it to me I said, "Hi! My name is Robert Gogerly, and I've been sent to see you about joining the "Times."

"Come in," he said. "Yes, they contacted me about you. I have to tell you though, that we have no vacancies at this time. But if you work with me as an apprentice, I will see what I can do when a vacancy occurs. We won't be able to pay you, but you could consider it as training."

"That's fine," I said hopefully. I was going to work my butt off so that when a vacancy occurred I would have a shot at being employed.

The assignments he gave me were to report on Inter-School cricket, which was right down my alley. I attended most of the games in Kandy and being a press correspondent, was given preferential treatment at the games, with free lunches and afternoon teas thrown in, hoping for good press.

Sports reporting was my love at the time and I made my articles as newsworthy as I could, submitting them to Ben for approval. The trouble was when they appeared in the paper the next day it was under the banner of Ben Van Reyk. He was getting me to do his work for him and taking the credit. And he was getting paid for it.

This didn't work for me and I stopped being his lackey.

I had fallen for Jill and was a regular visitor at her house. Jill's mother was a dance instructor and she ran a dancing school from home.

I applied for a job at Miller's in Colombo and was invited for a job interview. This was the same Company my Dad had worked for before he left to join the Army. The vacancy was in the colour laboratory serving Kodak. Colour photography was in its infancy on the island and a chance for me to get in on the ground floor.

I was interviewed by a Mr. Heel, my Dad's old boss. Deja vu!

"Another Robert Gogerly," he said, as he introduced me to the laboratory staff.

"Show Robert the ropes would you," he said to the supervisor, Bryan, "and give me an assessment on him. Help me make a decision."

I was given a tour of the plant and shown the laboratory equipment, while they quizzed me and assessed my suitability.

Mr. Heel called me into his office.

"Well, young man," he said, "Bryan was impressed by you, and we may be able to offer you employment." He outlined the terms and the salary and finished by saying, "You can expect a formal offer in the mail, and we will await your reply."

I returned home with mixed feelings. Although happy to think I would be offered the job, I selfishly did not like the idea of leaving Kandy and my girl-friend. I was torn between emotion and duty, and emotion won. I decided to turn down the offer when it came. I was not happy with myself, but I still went with my decision.

I have often wondered how my life would have turned out had I acted differently. It would have been an entirely different direction for me, but I'll never know. It was another pivotal moment in my young life.

We had moved to another home on the northern side of the lake, at the end of a winding road, to a place called Ampitiya, early in 1958

Chapter Twenty One

Political tension was brewing in Sri Lanka. The proclamation of the Sinhala Only Act had made the minority Tamils occupying the northern part of the island uneasy. After some political manoeuvring, a conciliatory 'Reasonable use of Tamil' Act was passed, but tension persisted. In the spirit of Nationalism that came with the Bandaranaike left-wing Government, it was decreed all vehicle registration number plates bearing the English SRI preceding the numbers, would be replaced by Sinhalese characters. The Tamils in the north reacted immediately with a 'Tar Brush Campaign' - using black paint to block out the Sinhalese characters on number plates.

In Colombo, the Sinhalese retaliated by blacking out all Tamil street names, shop signs, advertising hoardings, and anywhere Tamil signs existed. No prosecutions were made because it was impossible to identify the offenders. The unease led to violence when D.A. Seneviratne an ex-Mayor of hill country Nuwara Eliya, was murdered in Batticaloa on the east coast. This triggered riots that spread throughout the country commencing when the Tamils attacked a railway station in north-central Polonnaruwa.

Retaliation was swift in Colombo and surrounding areas as Sinhalese gangs roamed the streets dousing Tamils in oil and burning them alive.

Sympathetic Sinhalese in the street where my cousin, Customs Officer Rex lived, took in a Tamil youth being pursued by a gang of Sinhalese. Not to be deterred, the gang set their house on fire, witnessed in dismay by Rex and his family, who were unable to do anything in fear that their own house would be set ablaze.

Arson rape pillage and murder extended across the country and continued unabated. A curfew was imposed from 6 p.m. to 6 a.m., followed by the declaration of a State of Emergency. Armed forces acted swiftly and the situation was brought under control. The curfew was lifted as the situation returned to normal.

I was just a hot- blooded teenager at this time and was visiting Jill at her home in Kandy one evening late in May. Oblivious to the time (as was often the case) we were making out on the sofa in the sitting room when her mother and step-father returned home.

"What do you think you are doing?" her mother asked alarmed. It was 6.15 p.m. – past the start of the curfew. "You'd better get on your bike, young man, and get the hell home." They didn't ask me to stay the night.

I cringed sheepishly, bade them goodnight, and with a quick kiss on Jill's cheek, got on my bike to make my way home. I had to cycle around Kandy Lake, leading to a steep winding road that led home.

I had just gone past the lake and was rounding a bend in the road when I heard an Army Commander addressing a troop of Army personnel before deploying them on their patrols.

My heart began to race as I dismounted from my bike, trying to look inconspicuous, as I slunk into the shadows by the roadside wishing to become invisible. I was inching my way forward at the edge of the road, when I heard a booming voice, "What the hell do you think you are doing?"

The Army Commander was glaring at me with a baton in his hand, and I cringed. (Again. That was the second time in the last half hour)

"S, s . . . sorry, Sir!" I stammered. "I'm just going home."

"You think so?" he said disdainfully, "Do you realise what time it is? You could have been shot!"

I tried looking contrite, my heart hammering in my chest. This was not going well. He then ordered me into the house, outside which this was going down.

"Get in there, get down below the parapet wall on the veranda and I'll deal with you in a minute."

I wheeled the bike into the yard and leaned it up against the side of the house.

I ducked down below the parapet wall as he had asked me to, not knowing what was coming next. He sent his troops on their designated patrols and I heard his boots crunching on the driveway. This was it.

He walked out on to the veranda and stood with his feet apart in his khaki Commander's uniform, still carrying his baton, tapping it in the palm of his hand.

"Now, explain yourself, young man. Do you realise what danger you are in? No questions asked you could have been shot."

I had to stop myself trembling. I took a deep breath before I spoke.

"S. s . . . Sorry Sir," I said again. "I was with my friend and had a flat tyre, and had to repair the puncture, and didn't pay heed to the time, and it... it... got late." (That was the best I could do.)

"And what's your friend's name?" he asked.

"Derrick, Sir."

"Okay. Get in the car. We're going to Derrick's. You can direct me. He backs you up, you go home, he doesn't and you're for a night in a cell."

"I...I'm sorry Sir, I lied."

"You idiot!" he said, "I should lock you up for the night but I reckon you've got the fright of your life. Consider yourself lucky I'm not taking you straight to a cell for the night. Get in my car and duck down below the level of the window."

I did not need to be told twice.

He drove me home, which was just five minutes away. I would retrieve my bike the next day.

When I got home my mother was beside herself with worry and fear for my safety.

"Where were you? I was worried sick, not knowing where you were, or what was happening, and if you were safe."

"I'm sorry, Mum," I said, and told her everything.

I would never to put her through that experience again.

Chapter Twenty Two

I needed work. My journalistic ambitions had gone west, and I had declined a good job impetuously. I had to prioritise duty.

Everyone I knew sought work in Colombo, so I moved in with my cousins Rex and Ruth in the southern suburb of Mount Lavinia. I took a course in Stenography which was a starting point for those who wanted to work in an office and learned typing (on a manual typewriter – that was all there was) and how to write in 'shorthand'.

While completing my evening course I secured a job as a sales assistant in a bookshop. It was a stop gap but it paid for my board and lodging.

Rex was my mentor, a striking young man, handsome, well built, and fit - he worked out regularly. He sported a little French beard, which suited him. He looked impressive in his white Customs Officer's uniform, with a peaked Customs cap. He was known as "Snow White" at the Customs because he never took bribes. He was my idol. His wife Ruth (also a cousin) had sparkling grey eyes wavy dark hair and was of medium build. They had two young kids, a daughter, Astrid, and a son, David.

A vacancy occurred at a Trading Company in Colombo. I applied and was successful in getting my first real job as a clerk in the Tea Export Department of Colombo Commercial Company. I was with them for the next six years, working my way up through the department in Shipping, Billing, and finally in charge of Marine Insurance.

When a vacancy occurred in the Sampling Section I approached the Chief Clerk, Clarence.

"Any chance of my brother Alex scoring an interview?"

"What can he do?"

"Well, he's completed his schooling at Kingswood College, and is looking for his first job, He's done his senior year in general studies and I'm sure he would be capable of handling the requirements of the job in Sampling."

"Ask him to apply, and I will interview him."

In a couple of weeks, Alex was working in Sampling, recording the results of the Tea Tasters, who graded the teas into various brands for export.

Richard found work in Kandy in a Construction Company, and Barbara moved up to help my Aunt Gladys, who was Manager at the Bandarawela Hotel, the only Hotel with reasonable accommodation in town.

The Gogerly kids had launched.

Jill and I were married in December 1958 and we moved into a house not far from where I was boarding with Rex.

Our eldest daughter Judy was born on the 20th of November 1961, and her sister Wendy, on the 24th of July 1964. They were red letters days in our lives and I remember excitedly telling everyone I happened to meet, of their birth.

Wendy was born in Kandy, where Jill was with her mother at the time. Wendy was just over a week old when she nearly choked to death on her milk. I wrote an article about it that was published in the Sunday paper. It went like this.

SAVED BY THE KISS

As I write, my little two-month-old daughter peacefully sleeps in her pram, and her two and a half-year-old sister is rummaging in my wastebasket singing. "Happy to be a bachelor boy . . . until my dying day."

My wife sits patiently darning a pair of socks. But for the "Kiss of Life," this little scene of domestic life might have been one of tragedy.

Wendy was barely a week old, the central figure in this drama of a mother who had only just heard of the "Kiss of Life" as a method of saving a life. She had only a vague and hazy idea of what it was.

BABY BORN

My wife, Jill, had taken our daughter Judy, to her mother's home in Kandy, where her second daughter was born at St. Bernard's Nursing home. Mother and daughter returned home well and happy and Jill had written to me that they were looking forward to coming back home to Mt. Lavinia.

Wendy had been asleep and had woken at 10.30 a.m. as usual. She was feeding contentedly, if a little too enthusiastically, at her mother's breast. She seemed to be drinking too fast and she suddenly seemed to gag and choke. Jill raised her onto her shoulder and patted her back, to clear her throat. There was no response. She turned the little one over onto her tummy, placed her on her lap, and tapped a little more vigorously.

Still no response.

Back on her shoulder. Tap, tap, Tap. No result.

Jill was worried now and she called out, "Mum! Hurry I need you, Wendy's not breathing."

By the time she came to the room Wendy's body had turned blue. But her face was white. She looked pale. Her little eyes rolled up dangerously and she was limp. Jill and Iris tried frantically to clear the block but without success. The servant was sent to the neighbouring Dispensary, and Iris called a neighbour over, a mother of three. They kept up their tapping, but Wendy remained limp, and her eyes were closed. There was no sign of life.

SHOOK HER

In desperation, not knowing what better to do, Iris held her aloft and shook her vigorously. The only result of this was that Wendy's head lolled to the side, onto her shoulder. Iris burst into tears. With little wisps of cotton wool, they cleaned Wendy's nostrils. Their hands were trembling so much they had difficulty getting the cotton into her nostrils. This wasn't the answer.

Jill was crying too. Then she remembered hearing about the "Kiss of Life." She placed Wendy on the changing table and leaned over her. She pulled her chin down with her right hand and breathed into her mouth, paused, and did it again, allowing Wendy's lungs to deflate after each blow hoping to revitalise and re-invigorate. She did this a few times, and then Wendy stirred.

A little colour came back into her cheeks. She spluttered and coughed, spitting out curdled milk that had blocked her throat and nose. Then suddenly she stopped and went limp again. Jill had stopped too soon.

She started up again, breathing, then pausing, and breathing again. Wendy came round again, slowly. Her colour was back, and she began to breathe normally. She opened her eyes, and at last, she started to cry. The crisis was over. Jill hadn't realised that she was supposed to pinch Wendy's nose closed when giving her the kiss of life. It must have been curdled milk that blocked her nose and gave the same result.

In the meantime Judy, realising something was seriously wrong, panicked with the rest of the adults crying out, "Wendy! My little sister Wendy! What's happening to Wendy?" She developed a fever and took two days to recover.

Chapter Twenty Three

Sri Lanka was changing. The post-independence stability of the right-wing United National Party (UNP) had given way to the left-wing Sri Lanka Freedom Party (SLFP) and Marxist parties of the sixties. Prime Minister S.W.R.D. Bandaranaike was assassinated by a Buddhist monk in 1959 and was replaced by his wife Sirimavo Bandaranaike in 1960 – the world's first female Prime Minister. Uncertainty was in the air as political manoeuvring for influence in Parliament was the order of the day.

One day I said to Jill, "Ever thought of migrating to, say, Canada or Australia?"

"I've thought about it," she replied. "Either would be a good place for the kids to grow up in. They certainly would have more options than here." A distinct preference for Sinhalese Buddhists in the job market made it hard for others. This was in keeping with the new Nationalistic bias of the SLFP.

Dad occasionally wrote to Mum and sent her money. But this was infrequent, and Mum's replies had to go through his mother in Australia. His letters too came via Australia. It was obvious he was hiding something, but there was nothing we could do about it. I wrote to Dad asking if he could help us to migrate to Canada. He replied suggesting that we try Australia as it was a younger country, and we had family there, but he wasn't able to help us financially. He even said that he had thought of settling in Australia and he said, "You write well, and with your flair for writing and my flair for business, we could set something up in Australia." He was dreaming, this never happened.

We applied to the Australian High Commission in Sri Lanka for approval to migrate and were approved. We were allowed one year to organise our move to Australia.

On the 27th of May 1966, we boarded the passenger liner 'Oriana' to start a new life in Melbourne.

On a cold morning on 5th June, the 'Oriana' docked at Station Pier in Melbourne. It was winter in Melbourne and we had come from tropical temperatures right into a freezing winter. Dad's brother our Uncle John, was there to pick us up and we were soon at Grandma's house in Moorabbin. We were warmly welcomed and met the rest of Dad's family the next day, Sunday, when they all came round for the usual Sunday lunch which Grandma put on.

My Uncle George was one of the first to arrive, and Lanny, Dad's youngest brother said. "Hi there. Surprised to see you, thought you wouldn't be able to make it."

"Come on Lanny, you knew Roger was arriving, and of course I'd come to see the bastard." I gulped. Nice welcome! I hadn't yet learned of the Aussie way of speaking and that it was just a term of endearment.

Before I left Sri Lanka I had written to a Company to whom Colombo Commercial Company exported tea and told them that I was migrating to Australia and enquired about the prospects of being employed by them. I had included a photo of myself so they could see what I looked like. I received a reply stating that,

"We don't know what vacancies there would be, but contact us when you arrive, and we can set up an interview."

They were a Distribution Company in South Melbourne, and I was lucky enough to be offered a position in the Accounting Department and started work with them within a fortnight of landing in Melbourne. I was with them for six years.

After a month with my grandparents, we rented an apartment in Hampton, a neighbouring suburb, and settled down to a new life in a new land.

Alex followed three months after us but settled in Sydney, New South Wales, a neighbouring State to

Victoria. He lived with his cousins, the McHeyzer's in a suburb of Sydney. After a short stint in the Railways, he joined a large Bank where he progressed his career to Managerial level over the years. He was married briefly, bur marriage did not work out for him.

Life was good in Australia. Judy and Wendy settled into school, and Jill found work as a clerk in a commercial establishment also in South Melbourne.

I bought my first car, a blue Volkswagen, while I was still learning to drive. I drove it home before I got my driver's licence, and, driving into our backyard too close to the fence, put a dent in the front and rear guards.

The guy in the next apartment took one look at my new purchase, put his finger on his chin, and said, "Tut, tut, nice one Robert."

We all missed Sri Lanka but appreciated the new relaxed lifestyle in Melbourne.

As time went on, we all advanced in our jobs, and the girls in school and, with family visits, and regular vacations in the country, and sports activities during the weekends, life went on and years went by.

One morning in May 1974, I received a cable from my sister Barbara with sad news. Mum had passed away after being admitted to the hospital suffering from a bowel infection. International phone calls were not common from Sri Lanka at that time, and by the time we heard the news, her funeral was already over. I was heartbroken and I deeply regretted that I had not been able to go back and visit her in Sri Lanka.

Ten years after we settled in Melbourne cracks began to appear in our marriage and when I decided to go back on a visit to Sri Lanka, Jill decided she didn't want to go back, so she took Judy on a holiday to Hong Kong, and I went back to Sri Lanka with Wendy.

Chapter Twenty Four

We were at Melbourne Airport and going through Security. The security guy asked me, "How much money are you carrying?"

"Fifteen hundred dollars," I replied casually. I didn't realise that at that time I was not permitted to carry more than a thousand dollars in cash when leaving the country.

"You can't take more than a thousand dollars."

"These are Travellers Cheques," I said. Travelers Cheques was the accepted means of carrying money overseas at the time.

He still suspected something was not right and I found myself being asked to, "Step this way, please," and ushered into an Interview Room.

There were two cops in the room and I was asked to extend my arms to the side as one of them frisked me. "Is this normal?" I asked, confused. "What are you looking for? I'm just going on a holiday with my daughter."

"It's a random check, won't take long."

"Oh," I replied and thought I'd be flippant. I pretended to 'draw' two pistols from an imaginary holster on my hips, extended my index finger as an imaginary gun, and said "BANG! BANG!" pretending to blow smoke from the barrel and twirl the imaginary guns around my fingers before returning them to their holsters. Wrong move. They were not amused.

I remember the plane approaching the airport in Colombo, I looked down through the window and watched the rows of coconut palms in a plantation, as the plane descended preparing to land. My heart swelled with emotion. This was my country! The land of my birth. It was a euphoric feeling that words can't explain. It would happen each time I went back over the years.

We spent a month with my sister Barbara and toured the island. Wendy had the opportunity to see all the places that meant so much to me growing up in such a different culture, climate, and geographic habitation than she was used to in Australia.

It was a memorable holiday and we hired a car, with a driver, as we explored my old haunts. We met my family and extended family in their homes and spent a week with Uncle Ric in his home at Seven Springs in the mountains of Bandarawela. While at Uncle Ric's we went on picnics like in the old days with my niece Susan, Barbara's first daughter, and cousin Moira, who was living with Uncle Ric. Wendy and Susan struck up a close friendship which has lasted to this day.

We visited my brother Richard who was working on a coconut plantation and spent an afternoon with him, his wife Gloria, and children Debbie, Dan, and Dave. Richard was the most talented of us three. He was the extrovert in the family, I thought Alex was the 'quiet one' (he kept a lot to himself), and I was the one in-between.

Richard was easily the most talented of us, He had a good voice and could play the guitar and sing, and had gigs at clubs around Kandy. He could make electric guitars, and he made and sold toys between jobs. He was also a tailor. He worked with an Engineering Company as a bridge-builder.

My sister Barbara was married to a Sinhalese – Padma and lived in a suburb south of Colombo with their children Deborah, Sharmalene, Priyanka, and Lalini.

Time passed quickly and it was time to return. This had been a nostalgic holiday and it was a wrench to leave and return to Australia.

While boarding the Air Ceylon plane on the first leg of our return flight, I was on the top step of the boarding platform, when I turned around and saw a crowd of people with their faces pressed against the wire mesh border fence, at the side of the runway. Richard and his family were there waving goodbye. Impulsively I said to Wendy, "Be right back," and raced down the platform steps and across the grassy edge of the runway, to the fence. I pulled off my wristwatch as I ran, and passed it through the fence to Richard, It was a goodbye present, and we pressed our hands together through the fencing, completing our goodbye gesture.

I raced back to the plane and had to face a furious Security Guard who called me every conceivable name for putting the entire departure at risk. He reminded me that passengers were not allowed to have any contact with people on the ground once they had passed through the transit lounge. I had breached this rule and there were penalties. As he said, I could have been passing anything to Richard and the Security Police could have been called to investigate. The flight could have been delayed, and I would have been responsible for it. As it happened, I was given a 'slap on the wrist' and let off with a warning.

Times were indeed different then!

An announcement was made over the public address system on the plane apologising for the slight delay in departure, blaming it on an 'indiscretion' which had now been addressed. The Captain was given clearance to depart and the plane taxied down the runway, picked up speed, and then we were airborne and on the way.

Chapter Twenty Five

The cracks in my marriage widened to the extent that it became too hard to reverse and we ended up splitting. We both moved on, and after some time met others and married again.

My second wife, Barbara, was a Charge Nurse in a large hospital. I was moving up in my career and had been appointed Chief Accountant and Company Secretary.

We spent our honeymoon in Sri Lanka, and Barbara met my family and experienced what it was like to live in a different culture, with all its customs and traditions. We did some shopping and on one occasion we were in a Jeweller's shop viewing sapphires rubies moonstones and emeralds. Barbara showed interest and the salesman displayed a moonstone on the counter at which were sitting.

"How much is it?" She asked. Before the salesman could answer his supervisor said, over his shoulder, in Sinhalese, "It is three thousand, but say five."

"Five thousand rupees," the salesman said.

We pretended to consider the price, turning the stone over to examine it.

"It's a valuable piece of jewellery," the salesman said, "It will look beautiful in a ring."

Then very casually I said, in Sinhalese, "Oh! So it's three thousand but you said five."

He was dumbstruck for a minute, then said, "You can speak Sinhalese Sir! I would never have guessed." Embarrassed and awkward, he had no excuse. His supervisor had beaten a hasty retreat as soon as he realised what was going down.

"No Sir, I made a mistake," he said lamely. "I would correct the price if you are interested." I didn't trust the three thousand either, so we left.

Our daughter Sharon was born on the 5th. Of September 1979, and Rachel on 14th.June 1981. We bought a house in Wheelers Hill, an eastern suburb of Melbourne, and Sharon and Rachel settled in well at Wheelers Hill Primary School.

We spent a holiday in New Zealand, touring the country in a motor home, and Sharon and Rachel had their first taste of life outside Australia.

Alex was on vacation with us when we got the message from Sri Lanka that Richard had met his death in a tragic accident. He had just passed his final Engineer's Exam and was returning to work on a river diversion project with Skanska, an Engineering Company, when he was overtaking a bus on his Honda bike, skidded, and went under the bus. It was depressing news of the devastating loss of a loving husband, father, and brother, at such an early age. He was thirty-nine.

Robert Gogerly

Richard

Chapter Twenty Six

It was a hot summer evening in February. Dinner was over, the kids were doing their homework, and Barbara was in the sitting room reading a romance novel. I whistled as I walked over to the stereo unit and put on Neil Diamond's "Hot August Night" and settled in a comfortable recliner. I stretched out my legs, and my arms above my head, yawning. It had been a tiring day and it was good to relax.

"What a day," I thought to myself, not speaking so as not to interrupt Barb's reading. I closed my eyes and was pleasantly dozing off when the phone rang. "Damn it." I muttered to myself, picking up the phone from the table just by the recliner, "Man can't get a bit of peace and quiet in his own home. I wonder whose calling?"

I put the phone to my ear and said, "Hello?"

"Hi," a male voice I didn't recognize. "You don't know me. My name is Mark. Is Robert Gogerly at home?" "Speaking," I said, "How may I help you?"

"Is your father's name Robert too?"

Huh! What was this about? "Yes," I said, "What's that got to do with anything?"

"Well," said Mark, "I'm here in Melbourne with your sister Mandy, from England and she would like to meet you. Would that be okay with you?"

We had heard through Grandma in Melbourne that Dad had another family in England, but that was hardly a surprise to us as we had guessed he was living a separate life when he didn't come back to Sri Lanka. But we never expected to meet them and this was an incredible surprise. I took a moment to take it all in. Then the full implication set in and I said, "Yes, of course. We would love to meet her."

"That's great! Mandy is so excited at the thought of seeing you."

We agreed that they would come over the next evening and awaited her visit eagerly.

The visit was an emotional one.

We greeted them as they came up the steps the front of our house. Mandy came straight to me and put her arms around me and we hugged. Then she held me at arm's length and looked hard into my face.

"My God," she exclaimed, "You look so much like Dad."

Mandy was blonde, had sparkling green eyes, with shoulder-length hair, and was of medium height.

"Come in," Barbara said. "Come in, sit down and tell us everything. This is incredible."

She brought out short eats and opened a bottle of wine, and we talked for hours.

We learned that Dad had married Mandy's mother Peggy (we didn't know this) and there were six in the family. Shane was the eldest, then there was Nick,

Sharon, Mandy, Rowena, and Melinda, who was the youngest at eighteen.

It was a lot to take in. I told her what it was like growing up in Sri Lanka, and noticed that she was teary.

"What's wrong?" I asked.

"It's sad that we had him, and he wasn't there when you were growing up."

She told us how they found out about us. Mandy and Rowena were going through the dresser in Dad and Peggy's room while they were out shopping one day, and they came across a snapshot of a little boy with the words, "To Dad with love, from Roger."

They waited impatiently for Dad and Peggy to return, and as soon as they did, they asked Dad. "Who's Roger? We saw this picture in your dresser and couldn't wait to ask you."

Sprung!

Dad passed it off nonchalantly saying, "Oh! He is my son from a previous marriage."

That didn't sit well with Mandy or Rowena. Mandy was determined to find out more. She knew Dad's family was in Australia, and, with Mark, she had come to Australia to find me.

During our conversation, I told her that Alex would be coming over any minute.

"Alex? Who's Alex?" she asked.

"He's my brother," I said. And I told her about our sister Barbara, and brother, Richard, too.

She didn't know that there was anyone other than me,

It was an evening of surprises.

Alex came over and we talked till well past midnight.

Mark and Mandy who had spent some weeks at our grandparents' in Moorabbin spent the rest of her holiday with Alex and us. They visited her Uncles and Aunt, and we showed them around Victoria.

One day she said, "You've got to come and visit Dad and us in England."

I wasn't sure. "He might not want to see us," I said.

"Are you kidding? He'd love to see you I'm sure. He's not getting any younger, he's seventy-five, you know."

The next time Mandy called Dad, she told him about meeting us, and that we would be coming over to visit them all in England. We joined in the conversation and heard each other's voices after forty-six years.

"Dad? (It sounded funny saying Dad for the first time in forty-six years) It's Roger your eldest son."

There was a catch in his voice as he answered.

"Roger! Oh my God, it's good to hear your voice. How are you son?"

"I'm good, and how are you?"

The conversation was awkward for a start but got easier as it went on. I told him that Alex and I would be visiting later that year.

Our heads were spinning after we hung up the phone.

It was all happening so fast. The past and the present were clashing. Our heads were filled with thoughts we never thought we'd have, and emotions were high.

As much as we looked forward to a reunion, there was an air of apprehension at the thought.

Dad walked around in a daze for the next two weeks.

We enjoyed the time Mark and Mandy were with us. Mark was a good sport and helped me make a video recording of the visit that changed our lives.

Mum never dated anyone even after she knew it was over with Dad. And when one of us told her he would never come back, she said, "I know, but I can always hope can't I?"

I don't know why that memory came back at this time, but it did.

Chapter Twenty Seven

And so it was that in August of that year Alex and I found ourselves aboard a Qantas flight to London. The flight took almost twenty hours, halfway around the world, with a stopover in Singapore.

As the plane started its descent into Heathrow Airport, we looked out of the window at the green fields below on our first visit to England, We touched down at 7 a.m., walked through endless passageways with crowds of other arrivals, picked up our cases from the moving carousel and cleared customs.

Then we walked to the arrivals area through the customs door. We saw Mark and Mandy in the crowd of people waiting to welcome visitors. Standing next to them was this old silver-haired man with wavy grey hair, slightly stooped, in a white shirt and beige chinos, looking towards us as we walked over to them. I remember thinking, 'This man is my father!' I felt no immediate emotion but a strange dullness. We were seeing him after forty six years, and thoughts whizzed through my mind, with mixed emotions, - none of them were love. We greeted each other with hugs and pats on the back as we walked towards Mark's car in the carpark still feeling strange and awkward.

Mark sought to ease the mood asking, "So guys, did you have a good flight?"

"Tiring," Alex replied.

I chimed in, "We're so glad to be here at last," and the tension began to ease.

Forty-five minutes later we were at Mark and Mandy's home in Thornton Heath, a typical London townhouse.

It was neat and compact with a small yard at the front and back and had two storeys.

They showed us to the spare room upstairs, and we came down after freshening up, where Peggy had set out sandwiches and tea. We settled down comfortably in the sitting room and were soon chatting animatedly. The catching up had started, and we all had begun to relax as the conversation flowed.

"I'll have to cook you some of my special curry." Dad said.

"That would be great."

"He makes a good curry," Mark said, "but hot!"

Throughout the day the other siblings arrived, Shane and his wife Vicki, Nick and Sian, Sharon, Rowena, and Melinda, the youngest. They had planned a party for the evening. We spent the afternoon resting in bed, after our long flight.

The party followed through the evening and into the night and we felt welcomed, as we got to know each other. It was strange at first, meeting Peggy who was just eight years older than I was, but the awkwardness wore off as the evening went on. By the time the party broke up, it was as though we had all known each other for years.

Towards the end of the night, we were all in the back yard and I said to Mark, "I'd like to propose a toast to Dad."

Mark gathered everyone together and said, "Six months, two weeks, three days and seven hours after he came into our lives, our Roger would like to propose a toast to Rob. Take it away Rog."

"Okay," I said, standing in front of the group, next to Dad on one side, and Melinda on the other.

"It's great to be here with Alex, and to meet Dad, after forty-six years - and all of you as well. Thank you all for making us feel so welcome. It's made a big difference to us. Dad has been on the 'production line' for twenty-three years, between 1938 and 1961 the years when his eldest (me) and his youngest (Melinda) were born.

(A ripple of laughter went through everyone and someone said, "Good for you Rob.")

I went on, "What you see here is the result of his efforts. And as far as quality **and** quantity are concerned, there's not much better." I raised my glass.

"Here's to you Dad!" Everyone clinked their glasses and sipped champagne.

We spent three weeks in England with our new family but we hardly had time to get close to Dad. Mandy was very protective of him and would never leave us alone.

Shane said, "Mandy you have to let them be. They have a lot of catching up to do." But it wasn't until our last evening that we had Dad to ourselves when Mark took us down to the local pub.

Through all the years growing up, Alex harboured intense resentment of Dad and said, "If I ever meet him the first thing I'm going to do is punch his lights out."

I was more conciliatory and said, "I'm not going to judge him until we hear him out. We have to hear his side." But when we finally met, Alex couldn't get enough of him, and I was not so sure he could defend himself.

He was sipping a glass of English ale and rubbing his hand on his chest, and said to us, "You boys must be wondering why I never came back all those years ago. It's a long story and I'd rather not talk about it."

Yeah right, I thought. Nice try Dad.

But it was our last night, and we had lost any chance of really catching up. Alex said, "Its fine Dad. Why don't we let bygones be bygones, we're here now, let's look to the future." And we all clinked glasses and drank to that. Later that night we all went out to a local Italian restaurant for our last dinner before we left the next day.

The next morning they were all there at Mandy's for breakfast, and the mood was sombre. No one had much to say, as we all felt the wrench at having to split from the close relationship that had been established, over the previous weeks between the two sets of siblings half a generation apart. The conversation was sporadic as we finished breakfast before all driving up in three cars to Heathrow airport to board our plane.

We were in the airport cafeteria before check-in and saying our goodbyes.

"Keep in touch," Mandy said.

"It's been awesome having you over."

"You bet," I replied, "You guys have to come over to Australia."

"I don't want you to leave," said Melinda, who had grown very close to me and helped me with the voiceover for a video I had done, of the trip. She had tears in her eyes, and I noticed a few of the others getting teary as well. Dad was very quiet and hardly said a word.

Then it was time to check-in, and we joined the line and waited to complete the formalities and get our seat allocation.

The boarding call was made. "QA Flight 8 to Honolulu is now ready for boarding from Gate 16. Passengers are requested to make their way to the gate lounge." It was time to go.

We said our teary goodbyes.

"Bye Dad, it was awesome meeting you after all these years."

"Take care you boys, be sure to come again."

Then we walked through to the security area to have our passports checked, and turned to wave one last goodbye.

It was over.

We felt flat and sad, after spending an emotional holiday with the English part of our family and establishing such a strong connection. We had not foreseen this for an instant.

We were on our way to Hawaii for a short visit on the way back to Melbourne. We didn't want to go.

The visit to Hawaii left us feeling empty and flat.

We visited Pearl Harbour and the s. s. Arizona Memorial re-living the Japanese air attack on Oahu Island in December 1941 as they entered the Second World War, precipitating America's entry and the eventual end of hostilities with the dropping of two atomic bombs on Hiroshima and Nagasaki almost four years later.

We visited the Diamond Head State Monument and Waikiki beach and went on a sunset dinner cruise, but our hearts were just not in it.

"We should have done this on the way out," I said to Alex.

"I guess. But we'd have been anxious to get to London and it would have been just as bad. Well, not just as bad, but you know what I mean."

"Yeah, I guess."

A few days later we were back home in Melbourne and the last month seemed like a dream.

I thought about Dad and how he had abandoned us all after the Second World War and forged a new life for himself in England. I just could not understand how he thought Mum would be able to raise four very young children on her own, at a time when the world was reeling after a cruel and devastating war. We hadn't heard his side of the story, but it was almost impossible to imagine how it could ever be justified.

I always admired Mum and my love for her was total, and now my admiration for her courage and bravery reached an even higher level than before.

Mum was an extraordinary woman, and now more than ever I regretted not having been able to go back and visit her in Sri Lanka after I had migrated to Australia.

Chapter Twenty Eight

A few months later Rachel came in after a play date with a neighbouring friend Stacey, with a tear in her white shorts, and a graze on her left knee.

"Rachel!" I exclaimed "What happened? Are you okay?"

"It's nothing Dad, I was just mucking around with Stacey and her brother on the lawn when their dog decided to join in and I got a couple of bruises. It's nothing."

Barb took her to the bathroom and dabbed some Betadine on the graze.

Sharon looked up from her homework.

"Dad. When are we going to see Mark and Mandy again?"

Rachel chimed in, "Yes, Dad, can we go see them again? Please, please, I miss them."

We were due for a vacation and that got me thinking.

To cut a long story short, at the end of their next semester we were in London again and Barb, Sharon, and Rachel met the Gogerly family in England. It was an exciting time for them, meeting the whole family, and they were happy to see their grandfather again.

We toured England, going to places like the Tower of London, Stonehenge, and Rochester Castle in Kent, traveling up to Chester, a walled city in Cheshire. Then we visited York with its city walls and the York Minster Cathedral with the famous Rose Window.

After a very pleasant visit with the family, it was off to Europe on a short whistle-stop tour, where Sharon and Rachel got glimpses of Belgium, France, Italy, and Switzerland, visiting places like Brussels, Paris, Rome, and Lucerne.

After a few days with the family back in London, it was time for the long flight home.

Sharon said, "Bye, Grandad. It was great to see you again."

"Bye kiddos. Now don't forget to write. I promise I'll reply."

We said our goodbyes and set off for the airport with Mark and Mandy.

Halfway through the flight, I was snoozing when I heard a Flight Attendant talking to Sharon and Rachel. I opened my eyes and saw her kneeling in the aisle as she talked. She was a good looking blonde with a petite figure and I guessed she came in at about five-eight in height. She looked good in her black and red uniform with a red scarf around her neck, trailing over her shoulder.

"Hi girls," she said, "On vacation or returning from one?"

"Going back home," Sharon replied.

"Oh, where'd you go?"

Rachel said, "We went everywhere! We met Dad's family in England and it was awesome. Have you been to the Tower of London? Oh.my God! The cruel things they did there. They cut people up, and some were tortured and locked away in those prisons for years. Did you see what they used to torture people with? Like the rack! Yuk! How could they be so cruel?"

Sharon chimed in, "And have you heard about the ravens? They clip their wings so they can't fly, so all they can do is hop around the grassy mounds in the Tower. It's said that if the ravens ever leave the Tower, London will fall. So they have been clipping their wings for hundreds of years."

"What if they forget?" Rachel asked.

"I guess they make sure they don't. And if they do, I guess we'll find out. We went to Paris! We saw a show at the Moulin Rouge - it was spectacular."

It was Rachel's turn again.

"You should have seen the hill at Montmartre, with its cobbled streets and those artists in their funny little pointed beards, with their cute French accents, and their paintings hanging on boards behind them as they worked."

They were on a roll and you couldn't stop them.

"And Rome! The Colosseum where they made condemned gladiators fight with lions in the arena while thousands watched from the stands."

"We saw the arena where Charlton Heston took part in that chariot race in the movie 'Ben-Hur'."

"Remember Lucerne, with those musicians playing those instruments like a long pipe?"

"Wow! You girls had an amazing time! Listen, it's almost time to bring out a meal, but after you eat, how would you girls like to go up and meet the Captain in the cockpit?"

"Can we? Can we really? Mum, Dad, can we?"

"Sure," we replied together. That would be an experience.

After an airline meal of pink salmon with mashed potato and green beans, followed by chocolate mousse and fruit juice, Debbie (she had told the girls her name) was back.

"Follow me," she said as she walked the girls to the cockpit on the flight deck.

They returned a few minutes later, gushing with thanks to Debbie.

"Thank you so much, Debbie. That was so cool. Mum Dad! We got to say Hi to the Captain. He was a very nice man. And oh! Man, the cockpit! It was bigger than we expected. And all those lights and instruments. How do they remember what buttons to push, what levers to pull? It looked so confusing."

They were on a high, and we guessed they would never forget that experience.

They eventually settled down to sleep. Hours later we were back home in Melbourne and life went back to normal.

Chapter Twenty Nine

Time moved on.

Wendy married Drew in 1991 and their daughter (my first grand-daughter) Monique was born on 5th August. Judy married Paul in 1993. Five years later Wendy's second daughter Shanti was born on 24th January 1998.

At Ferro, where I worked, we were installing a new computer system – an IBM System 36. Martin, the Finance Director and 2IC to Bob, who was the CEO, was not happy with the way Bob was handling things and went over his head to the big guys at International Headquarters in Cleveland, U.S.A.

Big mistake.

Bob called Martin into his office and said to him, with no preamble, "Martin, have you considered an alternative career path?"

"Are you telling me what I think you are telling me?"

"You got that right."

Goodbye Martin.

Martin was my ultimate boss but my chain of command was through my Divisional Manager, David. I worked closely with Martin though, and we went out to lunch on a Friday. "Rob, I'm yesterday's man," he said dejectedly.

"I guess going to Cleveland over Bob's head was not such a good idea."

"Yeah, I learned that at my cost."

His next job was at Australia Post and I guessed he wouldn't be making that mistake again.

I was at my desk one morning in March when the phone rang. It was the CEO. "Can you come up to my office please, Robert." I walked up to his office and tapped at his open door. He was standing at the window overlooking the street. "Come in," he said, turning to greet me, gesturing to a chair opposite his desk. I sat, as he moved back to his desk, and he did the same in a comfortable leather chair.

"How are things going in the Coatings Group?" he asked, steepling his hands to a point in front of him, his elbows resting on the desk.

"Couldn't be better, right now," I answered. "We just got the Johnson Brothers Account sorted out, and you know how much that means to our bottom line."

"Now to the reason why you are here. We need to appoint a Company Secretary, now that Martin's gone, and I'm offering you that position. You don't have to answer right away, think about it and let me know by close of day."

The Company Secretary was responsible for reporting on all statutory obligations, and this had been a part of

Martin's job portfolio. It would be a step up for me and I didn't have to think twice about accepting but I held back.

"Thank you for your confidence, Bob."

"Oh I'm sure you won't have a problem, Robert, after all, you were Company Secretary in your previous employment."

I was about to leave and was almost at the door when he stopped me. "One more thing, Rob. We also need a new Finance Director - the job's yours if you want it. Think about it and let me know."

That was a bigger appointment, he had kept it back as a surprise.

Finance Director? That would make me 2IC. What was there to think about? My heart was doing handstands in my chest but I played it cool.

"Oh wow! I didn't expect that. I'll come back to you by tomorrow. Thank you."

I left in a daze. This had come as a surprise and I needed to settle. I took a few deep breaths, walking on air back to my office in the Coatings Group building.

I accepted of course, and the next morning I told Bob that I would be honoured to join him on the Board of Directors. We were in his office, he was leaning back against his desk and I was seated in a chair opposite. The mood was relaxed, and he leaned forward, extending his hand. "Congratulations and welcome aboard." We shook on it, and he said, "Well, you'd better move into Martin's office."

News travels fast, and when I got back to my office my soon to be ex-boss shook my hand and said, "Congratulations Rob. You have my full support."

I had leap-frogged five Divisional Managers in my appointment as Director, and looked for signs of resentment, a tightening of the jaw, or tension in his grip, but didn't detect signs of any. The other Divisional Managers too seemed to be genuine in their congratulations. Maybe it was because I didn't play political games.

I was amused at the reaction of the staff. When anyone saw me approach he or she would slow down and hug the side of the wall till I passed. I thought I'm still the same guy I was this morning. Nothing's changed except a title.

We had a celebratory dinner at home that night, and I just got on with the job.

I thought it was time to take the kids back to Sri Lanka and show them where I was born and grew up - re-visit all my old haunts and share my stories with them.

The school semester would be ending soon, and after dinner, we were relaxing in the sitting room, I said, "How would you like a trip to Sri Lanka?" They were ecstatic. We had talked about this on and off recently, and it was time for it to happen. Hotels booked, flights arranged, we were ready.

PART TWO

"When all the tears have fallen"

Chapter Thirty

There was an air of expectancy and keen anticipation as we boarded a Qantas jumbo jet in Melbourne on that July afternoon in 1994. Barb and Judy were taking their annual vacation from their jobs as Nursing Administrator and Physiotherapist, my son-in-law Paul, from his job as Promotions Manager at Polydor Records, and Alex from his as Bank Inspector. Sharon and Rachel completed the party of seven. The only two missing were my second daughter Wendy, and my grand-daughter Monique, who was only two. Wendy had just started working for herself on the Gold Coast in Queensland and the timing didn't work for her. She had been to Sri Lanka with me on my first trip back in 1976.

We boarded the aircraft and walked down the aisle to our seats in a group, looking forward to the next two weeks. I was eager for them to see the different world and culture, the romance and beauty of the place where Alex and I grew up – and where Judy and Wendy were born. At last, they would be able to see, first hand, all the different settings of the bed-time stories I told them of things that happened when I was a little boy.

An announcement was made over the PA system, "Good afternoon, ladies and gentlemen. Welcome aboard Qantas Flight 11 to Singapore and Colombo. The flight will take six hours and twenty minutes. We are just waiting for the last of the luggage to be loaded aboard. We should be taxiing for take-off in about five minutes. Sit back, relax, and enjoy the flight."

A few minutes later QF 11 taxied down the runway, received clearance for take-off, the engines roared to life as we picked up speed, and we felt the thrust back in our seats as we became airborne.

We were soon up in the clouds watching the map of our route on TV monitors suspended from the ceiling in the centre aisle. We chatted animatedly amongst ourselves as the journey commenced. After a while the steady drone of the engines made me feel comfortably drowsy and I settled back in my seat and closed my eyes.

I took a trip back in time to my youth, and the many adventures we enjoyed as boys in the tropical mountains of what we knew as Ceylon.

One memory flashed through my mind - a cool September morning as we trudged along a wet mountain track some four thousand feet high, and waded through a cool mountain stream. The water was ice cool around our legs and we could smell the wet decomposing leaves on the track. We cupped our hands and scooped up water from the fresh mountain stream. As I drank the water ran down my chin and neck sending a cold shiver down my spine. We trudged on through the forest, aware of the water dripping from leaves all around us in the steady drizzle. We could hear birds chirping in the trees, and the gentle flapping of red and blue lorikeet's wings, as they shook the water from them and flew off swiftly from branch to branch through the dense forest.

Then I was in 'fast forward' mode as I reviewed the last twenty-eight years in Australia, the ending of my first marriage, and then my marriage to Barbara. I remembered the day Sharon was born and the sense of awe and wonder at her birth – the first one I attended. It was a deeply moving experience. Then, before her second birthday, the excitement and anticipation we felt when it was Rachel's turn to come into the world.

I recalled taking Sharon to the Moorabbin Hospital and seeing her bend over to kiss Rachel, Then awaiting the time when Barb and Rachel would come home from the hospital. We had shown Sharon heaps of love, especially at this time, as she was going to have to learn to share her limelight with her younger sister. We gave her extra cuddles - heaps of them. And, as excited as she was to see her little sister when Rachel came home with Barbara I think she was a little surprised that we brought her home. This was upsetting the equilibrium.

And so she experienced the first pangs of sibling rivalry. We had made a rule that she could have a cuddle any time she wished – no matter what. So, often we interrupted whatever we were doing for a three-way hug – as it was 'any time for cuddles'.

They grew from infants to little children and soon it was time for kindergarten, then Primary School. As they grew and learned their social skills Sharon tended to look after her little sister in the various rivalries encountered at school. We observed the various friendships they made as they moved through Primary School, and before we knew it they were both in Secondary College. As they grew they developed their character.

Sharon is the more gregarious of the two. She has deep blue eyes and long sleek walnut hair. There is a wistfulness apparent when you look into her eyes, and she sometimes looks pensive. When she smiles her eyes light up. She is tall and slender and has fair skin that tans easily in summer. She has a playful sense of humour and a love of practical jokes, sometimes a tease but with a very warm heart. Sharon makes friends easily, but her close friends are carefully chosen.

More than once a close friend would have to move house, or in one case migrate back to her home country, and the sense of loss Sharon would feel at these times was deep and distressing for a while. She once asked me.

"Why is it that whenever I get close to someone I lose them?"

On one occasion a friend of hers 'lost' seventy dollars from her house. Her parents decided that unless the money was replaced their daughter would be taken out of that school. The boy who took the many was a friend of them both. His parents left it to him to replace the money. Sharon did not want her friend to leave school so she lent the boy seventy dollars. We told Sharon that that was very noble of her, though she wasn't sure she would get the money back. She would give the shirt off her back to a friend in need.

"He's promised to pay me back, Dad. In any case, it isn't fair that Melanie is made to change schools because of this. That is why I gave him the money."

They graduated from Primary School in successive years and graduation night was a big event. The graduation ceremony was followed by a dinner for the students. I am sure all parents felt proud of their sons and daughters as they went up in turn, to be farewelled by the Principal, who wished them well and a successful future as they ventured out into Secondary School.

Afterward, they attended their first 'dance' in the School Hall.

Sharon tended to be a smart casual dresser while Rachel was slightly more formal. They chose their clothes well and dressed elegantly.

Sharon and Rachel developed a keen interest in the environment and both sponsored dolphins through the "Friends of Port Phillip Bay" organisation.

Now in High School, rivalries were getting intense as an interest in the opposite sex developed. They both enjoyed their schoolwork and Sharon excelled in Math from a very early age. Rachel threw herself into her studies from a very young age and enjoyed her various assignments and projects.

Like Sharon, Rachel has blue eyes and long soft wavy hair with blonde sun streaks. There is a glint of mischief in her expressive eyes that twinkle when she smiles. She has a soft face and a cute little pointy chin, and a body that is tall and slender. Her personality is cheerful and bubbly, and she has a ready smile for everyone, always full of fun and enthusiasm. She is fiercely loyal to her friends, and whatever her interest is, she is passionate about it.

Rachel uses the computer a lot and always wants to be one step ahead. She often annoys Sharon when we get home from shopping, when we're pulling into the drive, by claiming first use of the computer. "I'm first on the computer."

Rachel decided to excel in school and put one hundred percent effort into all her assignments. We always impressed on the two of them the importance of presentation.

On her thirteenth birthday, when I arrived home after work, she called out to me to show me a letter she received from her School Principal.

"Look, Dad. Look what I've got!"

She showed me the letter. It read,

"Dear Rachel,

Recently your co-ordinator, Mrs. Scott informed me of the excellent results that you obtained in your recent reports. Brentwood is proud of the work that you are doing. I am sure that you will benefit greatly in your education here if you continue with the fine effort that you have begun in Year 8. Well done! Your parents must be very pleased with your efforts. Yours sincerely,

John Ardley

Principal"

She was beaming and her eyes were shining. I felt so happy for her and hugged her tightly, commending her on what she had achieved. I was proud of her efforts and told her so. She accepted the compliment with modesty saying, "Thanks Dad, I wasn't the only one who received a letter, there were eight of us." I felt a warm glow of appreciation for her.

The next day when I came home she had written a reply, saying that she was happy to receive the letter and saying that she was pleased that the teachers at her school were there not only to teach but to go that one step further and encourage their pupils. It was an appreciative letter. And I was glad she had thought to reply with such sincerity.

Rachel was keen to study Marine Biology and she was also interested in Law. She had written away to Cook

University in Queensland and obtained all the relevant information on courses in Marine Biology and Law.

Whereas Sharon was not keen on saving, Rachel always saved her money and used it only on special occasions. Sharon had the attitude that when you had it you spent it when you didn't have it there was nothing to spend. Money was not that important to her.

The two girls had a passionate love of dolphins, and one Sunday we went down to Rosebud on a dolphin viewing cruise on the boat "Looking Good". They couldn't wait for the time when they would be old enough to swim with the dolphins. That was a special morning as we watched these beautiful creatures gliding gracefully through the water, making a slight slurpy sound as they surfaced in an arc before submerging again - quite a few of them riding the bow waves made by the speed of the boat.

Rachel had a particular interest in the aboriginal people of Australia. When we were up at Hall's Gap at the Jumbuk Aboriginal Centre, she nagged me until I bought her a didjeridoo (an aboriginal musical instrument – a horn) which she was proud to own.

Chapter Thirty One

Early in April, we decided to dismantle the above-ground pool, around which we had installed Mirboo timber decking, which the girls had outgrown. Mandy and Mark from England were over for a vacation and joined in to help with Alex and the rest of us. First to go was the decking, then we built a bluestone retaining wall on the western side of where the pool had been, using charcoal coloured cement from a nearby nursery.

Sharon and Rachel did most of the work on the wall and I could see the sweat glistening on their foreheads as they lifted the stones and placed them in position for cementing.

"It's coming along good," said Rachel.

"Yeah," Sharon replied, stopping for a minute and reaching for a coke on the nearby embankment. She slurped down the drink and brushed a strand of hair from her face. "Want some?"

"Thanks," said Rachel, taking the can from Sharon, leaning her head back and emptying the can.

Then we paved the floor with autumnal earthy 'Sandstone Red' pavers in a herringbone pattern. Everyone worked hard and the job was done by four o'clock on the second day. We stopped to examine it. It looked good, but there was a very slight dip in the centre of the little courtyard.

Mark said, "Well, we aren't professionals, and I think we did a bloody good job."

We had all worked together to create our little courtyard. I wasn't satisfied and didn't feel right about leaving it the way it was, with that little dip in the centre. As we stood around eating cookies and drinking tea, I looked over at Rachel and caught her eye. She was looking directly at me and I could read what she was thinking, "We've got to pull them up and re-lay them, Dad."

A short sharp shower of rain left a small pool of water in the centre of the newly completed courtyard. That settled it. We would have to re-lay the pavers. Over the next two days Sharon, Rachel, Barb, and I worked hard to complete the job. It was hard work, but it felt good. This time the courtyard was completely flat. We exchanged high fives and Sharon said, "Now I can study here in summer:"

"We couldn't have left it how it was, Dad." I agreed.

One day Rachel said to me, "Dad the newsagent is looking for paperboys and girls to deliver newspapers every morning. Can I?" I had told them that if they ever wanted to do this I would take them on their rounds in the car. I didn't want them doing it on their bikes at that early hour, before sunrise.

I said, "Sure, I'll drive you on your rounds." Because we were using the car, she was soon offered two rounds, and then three. This meant she would be earning sixty dollars a week. Most kids did just one round, so it was good money back then.

We would collect the papers at the Newsagent's about 4.30 a.m. and load them into the car. As I drove to each address Rachel would lean out the window and throw the rolled-up paper onto the drive.

I remember saying to her one morning, "Rachel, as you grow up, you're going to notice that people will take notice of you. I can see by the way you've organised your life that you're going to be recognised as a leader in whatever group you are in. This means that you could influence people. Use this influence wisely and carefully."

Her embarrassed reply was, "Shut up Dad!"

A few days later, also during a paper round, I said to her, "Remember the other day, what I told you about influence?" She did an eye roll.

"Yes, Dad."

"Well, don't forget Rachel, that some people are not as fortunate as others. But everyone has a role to play."

"Do you think I don't know that, Dad? Everyone has a part to play, and everyone is as important as the other in their way."

Then one day, as I was turning into Grandview Road, she said, "You know, Dad, how I said I wanted to be a Marine Biologist?"

"Yes."

"Well, I notice there's not much demand for them. So I'm going to become a lawyer."

"That's good. Do you want to be a solicitor or a barrister?" I explained the difference to her.

"Well, I want to do both."

"Fair enough."

That's my Rachel.

On another occasion, we drove up a steep drive and when Rachel threw the paper it missed the drive and fell onto a grassy embankment. As she went to pick it up, she heard heavy male groaning and grunting. Looking up she noticed a light through a small window in what could only have been the toilet. "You all right up there?" she called out. There was no answer.

Another day in Garnet Road, we missed delivering the "Age" at number fifty-two and I had to reverse quite a way to get there.

"Which house is it, Rache?" I asked.

"The one with the shitty letterbox."

We were already there, and standing by the letterbox well within earshot, was a little man waiting for the paper.

"Quick, hurry up, let's get out of here, Dad. He heard that!"

I was snapped out of my reverie by the arrival of our meal. I sat up, brought my seat back to the upright position, and pulled down the tray table from the back of the seat in front of me. It was time to eat.

We arrived at Singapore late that night and were greeted with a wave of hot humid air as we climbed aboard a taxi outside Changi Airport. The smell of grease and oil was in the hot air as we made our way through the noisy traffic, to our hotel for our overnight stopover.

The next morning we did some shopping and then it was back to the airport to board our plane for the three and a half hour flight to Colombo.

We reached the Colombo International Airport at about seven at night.

Chapter Thirty Two

Again I felt my heart flutter and my pulse race as I looked down over the palm-fringed approach to the airport and saw the lights dotting the roadway below as we descended, and touched down. We alighted from the 747 and cleared Customs.

We were greeted by our host and driver of our touring van, at the airport arrivals area. His name was Das, and he was friendly and welcoming. He must have been in his late thirties, was of medium height and build. He had an olive face, short dark hair, and prominent teeth. We were greeted with fragrant yellow and white frangipani garlands that made us immediately feel at home and enhanced our feeling of excitement. "Welcome to Sri Lanka! We are so happy to have you visit us, and rest assured I will do everything I can to make your visit pleasant and memorable."

We swapped some travellers' cheques for Sri Lankan rupees and boarded our tour van, a spacious comfortable air-conditioned Toyota. The drive to Mount Lavinia some forty-two kilometres from the airport and twelve south of the City of Colombo was spent listening to a brief history of the island and the current political situation.

The drive was slow but interesting. The road was littered with potholes, so it was not conducive to fast travel. Occasionally a stray dog would wander across the road in front of the van and Das would have to sound his horn and step on the brakes abruptly. The girls were entranced, this was something new to them.

"Dad!" Sharon shrieked, "That dog just walked out straight in front of us. He could have been killed!"

Das just smiled. "Don't worry," he said "You'll soon get used to it. We get that all the time. Just have to be ready for it."

We drove past quiet little seaside villages, the dwellings consisting of a mixture of mud-brick huts, interspersed with regular brick houses of Dutch and English vintage. Then we passed the fringes of Colombo and more contemporary suburbs on the way to Mount Lavinia.

Along the way people lined the streets, talking in little groups – with children playing hop-scotch or chasey on the side of the road. The atmosphere was one of relaxed leisure. The business part of the day was over, and families were relaxing after their evening meal. We guessed Mums were swapping yarns of how they had spent the day and catching up with all the local gossip. Dads were chatting amongst their mates and neighbours, making plans for tomorrow, and discussing religion and politics.

At intervals, near temples by the side of the road, candles in paper lanterns, or little lamps made of clay with wicks burning in oil with flickering flames, lined the road. The lamps were placed on low parapet walls, and the lanterns strung together between poles in the ground.

The Mount Lavinia Hotel was a charming Colonial relic of the British occupation of the Island. It was a large white building backing right onto the beach. White uniformed doormen stood stiffly at attention, with pith hats, a common sight in days gone by, now not seen except perhaps exclusively here, lending an air of old-world charm to the welcoming scene. Coconut palms were dotted around the premises and on the fringes of the beach.

The night was still young, so we left our luggage in our rooms and made our way out onto the central terrace.

We were poolside on the terrace, and as the blue water glistened under lights in the night air, our eager eyes took in the scene to the left of the pool. On a raised platform a troupe of Kandyan Dancers held the stage. Lissome brown male bodies, bare-chested, were adorned with metallic discs shaped to the contours of their shoulders and upper arms, and on their chests, threaded together with colourful beads. Sweat glistened on their bodies in the hot night air. Long pointed hats, bordered with tassels, swayed to the movement of the dancers' heads as they danced to the rhythm of cylindrical drums draped around their waists. White robes, waist-high, tapered down to bells around their ankles.

Knees bent, feet splayed wide apart, they tapped first one foot after the other, to the throbbing beat of tautly stretched cowhide, and whirled around in a frenzy of graceful movement as the beat quickened.

Dom-de-dom, DOM. Dom-de-dom DOM, went the drums as the dancers beat a racing rhythm with their drumsticks. Heads bobbed, seemingly affirmatively, and the tassels hanging from their pointed hats swayed crazily as the dancers whirled around and around, faster and faster.

Long metal posts held lighted copra torches behind the dancers. Flames leaped skyward and black smoke twirled up in willowy threads towards the night sky filled with myriads of twinkling stars. The oily smell of a combination of smoke and burning coconut assailed our nostrils from the yellow flamed torches.

A full moon gave the scene a romantic light that brought back childhood memories. Memories of a first kiss on a night such as this – two teenagers on the beach awakening to new awareness. Maybe it was the throbbing drums that triggered the memory of 'that kiss' accompanied by the memory of throbbing hearts beating closely together. I remembered the arousing smell of her hair against my face on that magic night so many years ago. Our hearts felt warm with a nervous energy that surged through our young bodies as our breaths mingled, and we held each other close. And when we kissed, it was gentle and warm at first, before our lips parted and tongues tangled, passion flared and we seemed to melt into one.

The drums and the dancing stopped somewhat abruptly, bringing me instantly back to the present. I sighed as I came back down to earth.

I was beginning to feel tired, slightly jet-lagged, and the realisation hit me that I was hungry. It had been a long day.

"Anyone for a bite and a drink?" I asked, and there were positive responses from everyone. We ordered finger food and fruit juice from the wait staff on the terrace, as we sat around the pool. They brought out lightly fried chicken strips, spicy meatballs, and satay sticks with peanut sauce. You could taste the coconut in the oil used to fry the chicken. It wasn't exactly what we were expecting, but we were tired, and no one complained. We washed it down with tropical fruit juice, as we lay back and relaxed on the lounges by the pool.

Judy, Sharon, Rachel, and I walked along the ramparts on the outside of the pool overlooking the white breakers lashing against the rocks on the beach below, with a hiss as the waves broke and sank into the sand in the glow of the moonlight.

Sharon said, "Dad, it's beautiful! I had no idea it would be as beautiful as this."

There was a feeling of magic and anticipation in the air. They were all here in Sri Lanka to see where their Dad had grown up. They looked forward to experiencing first hand, a little of all those places they had heard so much about in bedtime stories I had told them all. We were all looking forward excitedly to tomorrow and the rest of the vacation.

Chapter Thirty Three

The next day was typical – hot and humid. We visited my sister Barbara and her family at Moratuwa. After catching up with all the family news, we drove to Colombo in the afternoon and I took Judy to the little Private Hospital where she was born. It hadn't changed much.

Colombo was much more crowded and bustling than we remembered it when we left to settle in Melbourne twenty-eight years before. The houses lining the streets had colourful flower beds and little patches of lawn between the front door and the street. Now that had been replaced in increasing numbers by zinc sheeted extensions to the front of the house. The streets seemed to be narrower than we remembered.

It was unnerving to be stopped at various checkpoints and at the entrance to the hotel, to have the Police or Army personnel go round the van with mirrored poles searching under the vehicle for bombs that may have been planted by Tamil Tiger terrorists, who were waging a civil war against the Government. Hostilities at that time were mainly in the northern part of the island, but there had been sporadic attacks in the south and security was tight. The locals seemed to take these precautions as a normal part of everyday life and we just had to get used to it.

The Tamil Tigers were crusading for the establishment of a separate State in the north of the country in the wake of the Nationalistic bias towards the majority Sinhalese Buddhist population. This was never going to happen.

After dinner that night, we were relaxing on the terrace.

"Anyone for a game of pool?" Paul asked looking around expectantly.

Alex put down his drink of tequila and said, "Count me in," and rose to join Paul.

Barb was doing a crossword in a hotel magazine. "What's a four-letter word for a boast and a bird?" "That's easy," said Judy twisting a bracelet on her wrist. "Crow."

"Should have known."

"I think I'll join the boys in the pool room."

Judy headed off after Paul and Alex.

Sharon and Rachel were just coming out of the pool. Sharon wore a green one-piece swimsuit and Rachel a similar one in bright blue.

Water dripped from under their white swim caps onto their foreheads. They draped towels around their shoulders and joined us at the table.

"Looking forward to tomorrow, Dad. Can't wait to see Kandy, your old home town."

"Me too honey, can't wait to show it all to you. Been waiting a long time for this."

"Can we climb Hantane, that mountain you've told us so much about in Kandy?"

"We'll see, girls. Depends on how we go for time. It will take about half a day but let's try to fit it in."

"That'll be great, Dad. I'd love to get to the top and have a look around, just like you did when you were a kid."

The next morning I woke early in the room I shared with Alex. Barb, Sharon and Rachel were in the room on our left, and Paul and Judy on our right.

I could hear the sound of the sea as the waves broke and rolled into the shore outside. I rose, stretched lazily, and walked out onto the balcony in the already warm morning air. I leaned over the rails and watched the waves as they hissed on the sand below.

I recalled a time when I carried my four-year-old cousin David around my waist and his six-year-old sister Astrid astride my shoulders as I walked into the surf for a morning swim. I leaned across at the corner of the balcony and said gently, "Shaz, Rache, - do you want to go for a walk on the beach?" No answer.

After showering and changing my boxers for a light blue cotton shirt and beige shorts, I went over and knocked on their door. Barb let me in and I walked over and sat on Rachel's bed.

"Morning Barb."

"Morning Rob, sleep well?"

"Always" I replied,

"You?"

"Like a baby" she replied.

Sharon was awake. "Morning Dad"

"Morning love. Hey Rachel, wake up."

Rachel stirred and surfaced from her sleep.

"Thanks for waking me. I was enjoying my dream."

"Any time, Rache."

After a morning swim in the pool, I walked down to the restaurant with Barb for breakfast. Sharon and Rachel joined us as we stood in the line waiting for a seat. We looked across at the wing where our rooms were and saw Paul walk out onto the balcony and stretch. He was naked and didn't realise that he could be seen.

"Stop bragging and get back in your room," I yelled.

He couldn't hear me for the sound of the waves, but he went back in, and a few minutes later he and Judy joined us for breakfast.

Breakfast was a smorgasbord of fruit juice, tropical fruit, cereal, and local fare. I filled a glass with passionfruit juice, which was a childhood favourite. One of the wait staff came over to our table with tea and coffee. I spoke in Sinhalese.

"Ayu bowan (Greetings), May amba ithi la the?" (Are these mangoes ripe?)

He was surprised that I spoke his language until I told him that I was born in Sri Lanka and grew up in Kandy. The locals didn't guess that I knew Sinhalese, and the word soon spread. They wanted to hear me speak. As they came around and joined in the conversation I could see by their sincere smiles and the sparkle in their eyes that they were as excited as I was. My being able to converse in Sinhalese made me feel a kinship with them and a comfortable sense of belonging. I felt their friendship and hospitality as we chatted light-heartedly. I told them of my boyhood days in Kandy, how I had left in 1966, and of all the changes I had noticed. They listened intently and joined enthusiastically in the conversation.

One young waitress, a pretty olive-skinned girl with bright shiny eyes and long black hair in a white uniform with puffy sleeves, tested my Sinhalese when she asked about my family, and our holiday. I did my best, and my vocabulary was just enough to see me through.

I filled a plate with some of the local fare - string hoppers (a mixture of steamed flour and water made into 'rounds' that looked a lot like vermicelli) and took it over to our table. This was accompanied by a coconut salad (sambol) made with grated fresh coconut mixed with finely diced onion, lemon, salt, and a light sprinkling of chilli. This was followed by cups of freshly brewed Ceylon Tea.

Rachel went over to the hotel shop to get some postcards of Sri Lankan scenes to send back to her friends in Australia, so they could see some of the beauty of the place.

Chapter Thirty Four

Our tour driver Da, had requested that we leave at seven in the morning for Sigiriya, a historical rock citadel 120 kilometres away in the central part of Sri Lanka. Being on vacation we didn't want to wake that early and said we would be ready by nine. And that's when we loaded our luggage in the touring van and took off on the first leg of our tour.

As we joined the morning rush hour traffic (shops opened at ten) we soon realised why Das had suggested a seven o'clock start. It was snail's pace traffic.

On the way, I asked him to stop at an electrical shop so I could pick up a connector for my Sharp video camera. We pulled over and I alighted. As I waited by the van for a break in the traffic, Das looked at me impatiently as if to say, "Why don't you cross the road?" But there was no way I was going to weave my way through the mass of cars buses and taxis, madly sounding their horns on a jam-packed roadway, as some locals were doing. I waited and waited for a break, and eventually was able to cross safely.

If I had only known.

I noticed as I came back to the van, that Rachel had my video camera and was filming my return across the road.

We were on the way again. I sat in front with Das, and there was laughter and singing in the van, and I remember thinking how happy we all were. Leaving the outskirts of Colombo we were soon heading towards the hills in the distance, the road winding through rice paddies (we called them paddy fields) and tropical vegetation. As we approached a little village called Gampaha we noticed a silver bus with red painted stripes across its centre, in front of us, with its destination displaying "DANKOTUWA". After some manoeuvring, we overtook the bus.

If only we knew.

A few minutes later Das asked us if we would like to stop at a wayside fruit stall and try some fresh pineapples. We said yes, and he pulled up at a pineapple stall. The pineapples were set out in neat rows on the shelves of a small thatched hut, and the lass in the stall sliced pineapple and plated it for us to taste. Rachel took a bite of the sweet yellow fruit and said, "This is the sweetest pineapple I've ever eaten!"

Barb wandered down in front of the van to take a picture of a buffalo in a rice paddy. Alex and Judy walked in the opposite direction – behind the van, up a slight incline in the road to another fruit stall. Sharon stayed in the van – she didn't like pineapples. Paul and I were on the side of the road, just in front of the van, which was about four feet away from the stall. Rachel was talking to the girl in the stall.

I heard a swelling of voices and looked up behind our van. A group of villagers were a few feet away from us behind the van and were talking animatedly. A bus had veered off the road, failing to take a right-hand bend about fifty metres behind us. It was on the shoulder of the road bearing down on us.

I must have blacked out for a second because the next thing I remember was the bus almost in line with our van, on the left of it, on the shoulder of the road. I remember thinking, "If I don't move I've had it," and then I yelled at the top of my voice, "GET OUT OF THE WAY!" and stepped in front of the van. Later Paul said he was in front of the van too, but I don't remember seeing him there.

I heard the tyres crunching on the gravel on the shoulder of the road. The bus grazed the side of the van and I heard the grating sound of metal against metal, and the sound of breaking glass as the side mirror of the van was ripped off its moorings. I smelled the harsh smell of burning rubber and hot metal. Then I heard the sound of crashing timber as the bus ploughed through the pineapple stall and came to rest at an angle against a banana palm.

A crowd of people had made their way towards us while this was happening, their voices rising to a crescendo. I looked wildly around for members of the family. I seem to remember seeing them looking at the bus leaning at an angle in the ditch and thinking, 'that was close.' Everyone seemed to be there, but I had a dreadful sense of foreboding – and then I heard Paul say, "Where's Rachel?"

That's when I lost it. Panic gripped me as I willed her to be okay. "Rachel, Rachel! WHERE'S RACHEL?"

Then with fear and panic clutching at my wildly beating heart, I bent over and looked under the bus. To my eternal horror, I saw my little daughter under the bus on her side, her knees slightly hunched up, her shoulder pinned under the rear wheel, pale and inert.

"Oh no! RACHEL, NOT RACHEL!"

I felt sick in my stomach and a cold fear in my heart. The sweet smell of smashed pineapples wafted across the humid air. I was sweating profusely. I could smell my sweat. I wanted to vomit, and I was choking. I felt completely disoriented. For a moment I didn't know where I was. It was as if I was in a nightmarish dream. Time seemed to stop.

I heard someone say, in Sinhalese, "There's life in her – she's breathing!" I thought, "Thank God. Please God, make her all right."

My mind willed her to be okay. My God! I hope she's okay. My heart cried out in dread and anguish. 'What the hell is going on? How can this be happening? No! It's not real. It's a crazy nightmare! I want to wake up!'

There was a tight knot in my chest, in my stomach. I was tense all over. I could feel my heart thumping in my chest. I felt completely powerless – so utterly helpless. My breathing was shallow and rapid. I rushed over to the other side of the bus still in a state of blind panic. Barb was frantic. She was crouching by the back wheel, scraping away the dirt by the banana palm near Rachel's shoulder.

I think Alex, (or was it Paul?) and Sharon and Judy were there, standing by the ditch and we were all trying to push the bus up, and away from Rachel, so we could free her, I remember thinking, 'How the hell do we think we can push this bus up by ourselves?' I walked back to where the crowd had gathered and asked for help. The passengers from the bus were there, but the driver had fled,

I found myself talking in fluent Sinhalese – I had no idea where this came from.

"Please help us, that's my daughter under the bus. Oh, please help to push the bus up and away from her! Would you please help? My daughter! My daughter!" But they were already pushing. More people gathered around talking wildly amongst themselves and pushed and pushed.

I heard someone say, "It's no good. We can't move it. We'll have to push down."

Barb said, "Don't let them push down, not the way Rachel is. See if there's a jack available to raise the bus away from Rachel."

I screamed, "NO, NO, not down. Her head is almost against the wheel. It's got to be UP. You could crush her head if you push down. Please! PLEASE!"

And finally, with one great heave, the bus was raised just long enough for those helping to lift the pale and almost blue figure of Rachel away from the bus. They carried her to a Volkswagen Kombi van with two Catholic priests who had stopped to see what was going down.

As they carried Rachel I noticed a cloverleaf on the closed lid of her left eye. My darling Rachel, my poor little angel, please be all right. I love you, Rachel.

The priests had offered to help, and Barb, Judy, and Paul helped get Rachel into the Kombi van, and they headed off to the nearest hospital.

I felt stunned, lost, forlorn, hurt, bewildered, angry, sad, trembling with apprehension. I found Sharon and Alex looking much like I must have looked. A car appeared from somewhere and a tour operator asked us to get in. I remember slamming my right fist into my left hand and saying with a lot of pent up emotion, "Fucking bus driver!"

In the car, heading towards the Colombo General Hospital Sharon said, "She's going to be all right. She's the best!"

Alex said, "Let's get the best medical attention for her, and then let's get her out of here and home – fast."

I kept thinking, 'Please God make her all right. I'll do anything you ask – just let her all right, please God. Please.'

It seemed an eternity before we reached the Emergency Department of the Hospital in Colombo.

A long line of people wound its way to the gate. Alex wanted to join the line. I said, "Bullshit, come with me."

"Take it easy," Alex said, "You can't expect them to let you jump the queue."

"Fuck the queue," I replied, as I entreated the official at the gate to let us in. "This is an emergency! My daughter's been in an accident. I have to get in to see if she's all right," and I opened the gate and walked in. Sharon and Alex followed me. The official must have seen the devastation on my face. He didn't stop us. We reached the Emergency Ward.

"Was there a foreign girl brought in?" I asked. "The victim of a road accident?"

A blank stare in reply. "She's not here yet."

"Then where is she?"

The Tour operators were again by our side, as if by magic. They had been in touch with their Head Office on mobile phones. Rachel had been taken to the Gampaha Hospital, and they were now on their way to Colombo.

"It's best if we take you to our Headquarters. You can wait there for news. It's only a short distance up the road."

At the Hemtours Head Office the Tour Director, Lakshmi, greeted us. "Don't worry, we have all the best medical help on standby. Your daughter will be given the very best medical attention available. We have alerted the best specialists to be on standby."

"Thank you, Lakshmi. Please spare no expense. She's got to be given the best there is."

Then came the intolerable wait for news. There were no mobile phones in the car bringing Rachel to Colombo. We waited in a Conference Room and I began pacing restlessly. We seemed to be waiting forever.

The phone rang.

Lakshmi picked it up and held it to her ear, "It's for you."

It was Paul at the Emergency Ward.

"Rob, it's no good, we did our best. We did all we could, she's gone!" His voice broke. He was sobbing.

Barb came on the line. "Rob, we've lost her, come over quickly."

I put the phone down. The three of us looked at each other.

"Oh! No, oh! No! WHY?" I exploded in a blind rage.

The Hemtour people were understanding. With sinking hearts, we went back with them to the Hospital. Paul and Judy looked haggard. Barb was slumped on the floor with a blood-stained top. Paul had no shirt on.

Sharon, Alex, and I walked into the ward.

We hugged.

We sobbed.

There, lying on a metal-topped table lay my beautiful thirteen-year-old daughter looking peaceful and serene. There was not a line on her face. I looked at my precious little girl. Her eyes were closed. They would never open again.

I leaned over and kissed her on her forehead and cheeks. Tears poured down my face. I will never forget the scene and the despair I felt as I sobbed and sobbed, my breath catching as my body was wracked with sadness, looking down at Rachel.

Then I was filled with uncontrollable rage.

"WHY?" I screamed out, "WHY? She was only thirteen years old. Goddamn it – WHY, WHY, WHY? She has done nothing wrong. SHE WAS ONLY THIRTEEN YEARS OLD – SHE HAD THE WHOLE WORLD IN FRONT OF HER! What have WE done wrong?"

I felt a burning sensation in my chest. I was to feel this often in the coming months. No words can explain the sense of devastation and disbelief we all felt. It was a despairing feeling of powerlessness, of being trapped in a black gloom from which there was no way out.

Then I paced around the sparse ward, thumping my closed fist into its metal walls. Screaming in a blind rage. I was suddenly throwing anything I could lay my hands on, instruments, utensils, containers across the ward. (Sharon told me later that this freaked her out, - she had never seen me violent before.) It didn't make me feel any better. A despairing Barb said, "Calm down Rob. That's not going to do any good."

The Hemtours people drove us to the Inter-Continental Hotel, where they had booked us in. We were a sorry sight as we checked in, in crumpled clothes, Paul's and Barb's blood and vomit stained, Paul bare-chested.

I remembered the crowd at the scene of the accident. After Rachel had left, they were so enraged at what had happened, they rolled the bus over into the rice paddy, in a gesture of frustration and empathy with us. We felt humbly thankful for their spontaneous help. I remember seeing the destination displayed at the back of the bus.

It said, DANKOTUWA.

It was the bus we had overtaken just outside Gampaha.

Chapter Thirty Five

We were booked into three rooms on the fourth floor, which weren't adjacent to each other. Sharon and Barb shared one, Paul and Judy another, and Alex and I the third. We gathered in the centre one, Judy and Paul's.

We stared vacantly at each other, words failing us momentarily. Then we cried uncontrollably, trying vainly to comfort each other. We paced the floor like zombies caught in some terrible nightmare. Surely we'd wake up and find it was all some horrible dream. If only.

Then we started to piece together from different viewpoints – what had happened in a few short sickening minutes. We were all confused and everything seemed intermingled. This is how each of them recalled events, from their different perspectives.

Alex and Judy had wandered up behind our van and had checked out some other fruit stalls, and had taken some photos. They suddenly became aware of a babble of voices and saw a crowd gathering near our van. Alex said, "What's going on? Don't tell me Rob's got into an argument with someone?" And they walked down to where the van was.

Sharon remained in the van. She heard me scream, "Get out of the way!" and step out in front of the van, and saw the bus whizz past the van on the left, grazing it and ripping out the side mirror. The stall was in its path and was soon a pile of shattered rubble.

Paul was standing outside the van. I don't remember seeing him in those short terrifying minutes. He agonised for weeks on the fact that he should have been able to dive across and push Rachel out of the path of the bus. He remembered looking up and seeing the terrified driver who appeared to be pumping away at the brakes in a futile bid to stop the bus. The brakes weren't working. WHY THE HELL DIDN'T HE

SOUND HIS BLOODY HORN? Maybe that wasn't working either.

Barb said she had walked across in front of our van to photograph some buffaloes in a rice paddy. She heard the commotion, turned, and saw the bus travel alongside her in the ditch. She heard the crash of timber as the stall was demolished and parts of it were dragged along. Barb came towards the bus in dread, and it wasn't long before she saw Rachel pinned under the back wheel. Soon she was on her knees, scraping furiously at the dirt near the wheel – trying to free her.

Then suddenly she felt the strong presence of Rachel over her shoulder.

Barb's nursing instincts took over as the others gathered round to help to try to push the bus away from Rachel. Barb was trying to get at Rachel, to get her free. Then all the passengers were lined up and pushing as hard as they could. Events seemed to be happening in two dimensions. On the one hand, everything seemed to be happening in the twinkling of an eye, like a video in fast forward. On the other hand, when thinking back, everything seemed to be happening in slow motion, and suddenly there was Rachel in the Catholic priests' van with Barb, Judy, and Paul, and a decision was made to head for the nearest hospital. That was at Gampaha.

The nightmare that followed was a blur. Barb and Judy gave a recollection of events. This is how I recall what they said . . . Rachel on a stretcher, being carried into the Gampaha Hospital . . . A doctor seated behind a desk . . . "Please help us, I know we are of a different race, but my daughter's been in a serious accident. Will you please help us?"

No response . . .

He just sat there not saying or doing anything . . . Barb snapped. "You're not DOING anything! You're just sitting there!". . . "Then I will just do nothing". . . Barb, Judy, and Paul just walk away in disgust, asking for her to be to put her back in the van . . . "We've got to get some help.". . . Someone sees them, says to bring her up in the elevator . . . they enter a ward . . . a more

concerned nurse and doctor pay them attention . . .
Rachel arches her back . . . they stabilise her . . . it's all
primitive equipment.

"You'd better get her to Colombo General   Hospital."
. . . Rachel's pulse is very faint . . .   on another stretcher
to the 'ambulance' . . . - just a van, with a siren . . . the
drip is woefully inadequate . . . then while transferring
her from the stretcher to the ambulance she stops
breathing – there is no pulse!

Frantic work in the ambulance – a confused nurse is not
much help . . . "Rachel, hang in there, we're doing our
best." (Paul).

Barb and Judy take their places, Barb with CPR, Judy
with cardiac massage . . . Please God help . . . Rachel
vomits . . . breakfast and pineapple. . . Rachel is turned,
her mouth cleared with fingers . . .   then they start
resuscitation again . . . there is a faint pulse.

Barb's top is blood and vomit soiled . . . the drip
stand slides across the van floor. Everyone is thrown

off balance as the van swerves to avoid traffic . . . they finally reach the Colombo Hospital . . . Rachel is taken into ER . . . a long anxious wait – then it's over.

Just over an hour ago, she was a warm vibrant teenager, full of fun, humour and Joy-de-Vivre, the whole world in front of her. A few brief moments and heaven turns to hell. Where was God when we needed Him?

The doctor never even goes near them. He just looks at them, then turns and walks away. Paul chases him up the corridor, but to no avail. Barb and Judy walk back to ER. An orderly and a nurse are already applying jaw bandages and tying Rachel's feet together. Barb goes berserk, "Get rid of them! Her father and the rest of the family aren't even here yet!" She rips them off and throws them on the floor.

Time passes in hour-long minutes.

Barb is sitting on the bed, rocking back and forth. "I want her back! I want her back." We all do. We're all sobbing again. We've got to go on. We've just got to go on.

Then we're playing cards. I drop back on the bed wearing a despairing frown. Judy notices and comes over and tries to comfort me – massages my shoulders. Judy's reaction is to keep her thoughts active. Her brain goes into overdrive. She doesn't stop talking, rationalising, analysing, planning, - anything but stop to feel emotion.

While we are all feeling lost and drained. Judy comes up with, "Let's think of the positives. Come on there's got to be some positives."

Positives?

"For God's sake Dad. She was hit by a bus! And yet there was not a mark on her. She wasn't broken. She wasn't broken, Dad. We saw no blood at the scene. There were no broken bones we could see. There was not a line on her face. She looked so peaceful. Dad, these are positives."

She was right. My beautiful daughter was right. God bless her.

What caused us most anguish was wondering if Rachel saw the bus coming and the horror she would have felt as it bore down on her, The girl in the pineapple stall sprang back out of its path. Rachel's path was bounded by the shelves of the stall. She had nowhere to go. We agonised endlessly on what she must have gone through. The girl in the stall said she was unsighted by the shelves behind her and didn't see the bus. We prayed that this was true. Then I figured that if Rachel didn't see it coming, she would have blacked out at the instant of impact and we prayed that she didn't feel pain.

Paul had been in a car accident in Denmark several years ago, and he told us about his experience. The car he was driving went out of control on a country road and rolled at impact with another car. Paul remembers feeling no pain at all, but suddenly finding himself above the car watching himself in the car as it rolled over. Then he 'came to' and checked himself by placing his hands all over his body, He seemed to be okay. He felt numb and unreal. He wanted a cigarette to calm himself, but he smelled gasoline and knew he could blow himself up. Then he lapsed into unconsciousness and woke up in the hospital. He had a ruptured lung, three broken ribs, and a broken neck, and he had difficulty breathing. But he said he felt no pain. We took some comfort from this.

We hadn't eaten all day and weren't hungry, but we had to eat, so we forced ourselves to go down to the restaurant for dinner.

Back in our room in bed, I talked to Rachel. "Rachel, I love you. If you're around Rache, just give me a sign. Some sign that you're around." A light breeze wafted across my face. I was to hear of a similar experience of a breeze across the face of a friend, just after she lost her sister in a car accident.

I walked over to Barb and Sharon's room. Sharon had become a tower of strength taking over a comforting role. "Dad, we need to get some sleep, you'd better try and do the same." Sharon had suddenly been deprived of her childhood.

I slept fitfully, and then it was morning.

The nightmare continued. The Australian High Commissioner visited us. He was gentle and understanding but we had to face reality. We had to cancel Rachel's passport. We needed to go down and identify Rachel in the morgue. And make arrangements to take Rachel back to Melbourne. Because she died in an accident, there had to be an autopsy. We couldn't bear the thought of that but we had no choice. Barb had to have a medical cause of death.

Barb and I went down to the morgue and had to face seeing Rachel lying in the morgue on a slab in what was like a giant filing cabinet. She still looked peaceful and calm. We felt a million knives twisting in our hearts, The Police were there, and we had to sign some papers. How many more statements did we have to make? We signed the stupid goddamn Police papers.

We saw the girl from the pineapple stall. She'd sprung aside – why hadn't she pulled Rachel away from the oncoming bus? We saw the driver of the bus. We felt nothing – just numb.

Back at the hotel we talked about a burial or cremation. Sharon said that Rachel had once mentioned that she would want a cremation with a wish that her ashes be scattered on Port Phillip Bay so she could swim with the dolphins. So it was a unanimous decision that it would be a cremation.

We made a pact that we would stick together until this was all over. We would see this through together, and we needed each other's support and strength.

Then came the calls to Brendan at the Funeral Director in Melbourne. He informed us that the coroner in Melbourne would not allow a cremation if death had occurred overseas and an autopsy had been performed. It was permitted in any State in Australia except Victoria. They would make a representation for discretion to be applied, but he didn't hold out much hope. This was the last thing we needed.

We had to make funeral arrangements. We wanted to make Rachel's farewell a celebration of life. We would include all the happy memories we had of her and play her favourite songs. We decided that we would do this our way.

The next day Sharon, Judy, Alex, and I attended the inquest. Even though she needed to know the cause of Rachel's death Barb did not want to attend the inquest, terrified that she would find that there was something she could have done that would have saved Rachel's life.

After an anxious wait for the Medical Examiner's report on the autopsy, it arrived. "Death was due to laceration of the liver," it said. There was no serious head injury. She wouldn't have stood a chance even with the best medical attention available. There was nothing Barb or anyone else could have done.

The courtroom was small, hot, and dirty. It was crowded and smelled of sweat and cigarette smoke. Two ceiling fans worked ineffectively in the humid room, just serving to spread the cigarette smoke. The buzz of voices in Sinhalese seemed to add to the heat.

A dark-skinned man in a shirt and a sarong (the local garb) on my right was chewing betel, which was a pungent peppery leaf. Rolled into this leaf was a white paste called 'lime' and a small areca nut – about the size of an olive? After chewing for some time saliva collected in his mouth. He put two fingers across his lips perpendicularly, and next thing a stream of red saliva shot out of his mouth from between his fingers onto the wall of the courtroom and dripped down the wall in a red streak. I looked around the room. There were more red streaks on the walls, in the corners of the room, and on the floor. Betel chewing was a disgusting local custom, not the chewing, but the spitting.

The inquest was conducted in Sinhalese, intermingled with English. The driver of the bus was unlicensed, and the brakes had failed. The driver and the girl from the pineapple stall gave evidence.

Then it was my turn, I wanted to ensure they got the story right so I lapsed into Sinhalese. The coroner commented that I spoke good Sinhalese. I told him I was born in Sri Lanka and learned it in school. He accepted my evidence in Sinhalese and even asked why the girl in the stall had not pulled Rachel to safety. We had been through that question a thousand times.

He returned a verdict of accidental death.

The driver of the bus, who had fled the scene of the accident fearing crowd reaction, had turned himself into the Police and was being charged with negligent driving, Not dangerous driving causing death. Yeah right!

The next afternoon we visited the funeral parlour where a brief service was held for Rachel before the casket was closed preparatory to her journey back to Melbourne.

We were booked in on a Qantas connecting flight to Singapore on Saturday.

The service was hard on us all. Before we got back into the car to return to the hotel, Barb suddenly rushed over to the fence and leaned over to dry retch.

"I can't do this, Rob." I put my arm around her shoulder and led her to the car.

Back at the hotel, we received a steady stream of visitors - old school friends I hadn't seen in twenty-eight years, who had seen the news in the local newspaper. My family visited us several times. Now we just wanted to be left alone.

We forced ourselves into the hotel swimming pool. We had to get some exercise. But it was flat and sombre. There was no spark left in us.

The next day was Saturday and we caught our flight to Singapore. The connecting flight had been delayed and we had to spend the night in Singapore.

The next morning I sat on a chair in the airport restaurant watching the others file in. I was still in a daze and involuntarily I looked for Rachel. I thought to myself, 'Where's Rachel?' Then the realisation hit me once again – I would never see her walk into a restaurant or anywhere else for that matter, again.

The flight to Melbourne was interminable, and I kept wishing that the plane would crash and that we would all die.

When we arrived in Melbourne my work colleagues David and Lee, along with good friends Herschel and Faye, were there to take us home. They had put themselves out to greet us and it meant a lot to us to see them there. They were there for us and we felt their support. God knows we needed it.

The drive back home was eerie and I couldn't stop the tears when we turned into Grandview Road and drove past the houses where Rachel and I had delivered the morning papers. When we finally reached home we found that our good friend Lorraine had flown down from New Zealand to keep Connie, Barb's mother, company.

"Rob, I'm so sorry," she said as we hugged. It was an emotional greeting for all of us.

I walked into Rachel's room and the tears flowed freely. I went down to the car and looked in the back pocket of the passenger side seat. Rachel's newspaper list of her last paper round was there. Seventy-five "Suns" and fifty- four "Ages" it read. I tore it to shreds, tears streaming down my face. That list was written by Rachel just nine days ago.

Throughout these traumatic days, Sharon had been a tower of strength. Her calmness and composure were remarkable. We knew she was high on endorphin, which our bodies produce in copious quantities to help us cope with trauma. She was repressing her grief for the time being and we felt she had been unfairly wrenched from her childhood and dumped in a no man's land between adolescence and adulthood. She remembered meeting an American guest in the elevator of the hotel in Colombo when she 'spilled her guts' as she said, and cried uncontrollably.

The house was strangely quiet. There was no life in it. When we were last there, there was a sense of excitement and vibrancy as we bade goodbye to Connie, Barb's mother, who lived in her 'granny flat' at the rear of the house.

Walking into Rachel's room brought a sense of warmth and a desperate yearning for her presence, and a sense of frustrating fear and apprehension of a future without her.

Wendy had flown down from the Gold Coast, so all the family was together.

Chapter Thirty Six

Lorraine had brought her daughter Kelly with her to Melbourne. Kelly was Rachel's best friend and was like a sister to her. We were close friends of the Stock family, Brent, Lorraine, and their children Matthew and Kelly. Matthew was a couple of years older than Kelly, who was Rachel's age. The Stocks had migrated to Australia, and Rachel and Kelly attended the same school. They had decided to return to New Zealand two years before these events, and we were glad to have Lorraine and Kelly come over at this traumatic time with their support.

Barb called another of Rachel's friends, Sharon Evans. Sharon told Barb that she had a dream that Rachel was in a car accident. When she awoke the phone rang. It was Barb calling to say that Rachel had not survived a car accident in Sri Lanka. It sent a shiver down my spine.

I had called my Secretary at work, Jenny, and asked her to contact a friend of mine, Cliff, who was a Pastor, and ask him if he would conduct Rachel's farewell service. He said he would be happy to do so.

Judy, Paul, Sharon, and Kelly joined us as we worked late into the night picking out Rachel's songs and appropriate poems to be read at the service. Sharon took a leading part in setting out the Order of Service and picking out Rachel's favourite music. It was also Sharon who worded the funeral notice for the "Sun" newspaper. We put together a collage of happy photographs on a notice-board for the foyer of the chapel. A CD with Eric Clapton's "Tears in Heaven" was ready for the occasion – the song he had composed when he lost his four-year-old son.

Brendan made repeated representations for us to have Rachel cremated. The coroner, who had the power of discretion, refused to budge from his stance. We made arrangements to fly Rachel to Canberra after the service, and Brendan even offered to drive there. An eight-hour drive across the State border. We also reluctantly left open the option of burial.

We were still in a daze and operating on 'auto'. It was as if we were not there. And we were all physically exhausted.

The morning of the funeral arrived we went down to the offices of the funeral parlour, adjoining the Chapel, and set up the collage of photos on a table in the foyer of the Chapel. At Brendan's suggestion, I called the radio station 3AW and took part in a talkback radio segment with the 'Champion of Causes' presenter Neil Masters. Neil listened to my story, took up the cause, and called the Coroner's office. Still a brick wall.

A kindly cemetery manager heard the conversation on the radio and offered to help out with a cremation. He needed us to obtain two doctors' certificates as to Rachel's state of health, and confirmation that they could attest to knowing Rachel, and her whereabouts when the accident occurred. We rushed to our local doctor who ran a clinic with her husband who was also a doctor, and we had our two medical certificates. The cemetery manager was sticking his neck out in agreeing to cremation, but he felt so strongly about the issue that he was willing to do so. We were deeply grateful.

About two hundred and thirty people crowded into the chapel, overflowing into the foyer area, to say their last goodbyes to Rachel. "Love is all around" was playing, and listening to this song would take us back to that moment in the months ahead. The music ended and people who had seats took them.

What follows is a transcript of the proceedings of a poignant "Celebration of Life" of our darling Rachel.

Cliff was at the Lectern.

"Good afternoon. On behalf of Robert and Barbara Gogerly and family, I wish to welcome you and thank you all for your attendance here today. We come together to bid farewell to Rachel Simone Gogerly who was born on the 14th of June 1981 and died as the result of an accident on 4th July during a holiday with her family in Sri Lanka.

I'm sure I speak on behalf of everyone here when I say to Barbara and Robert, Rachel's sisters, Sharon, Judy and Wendy, her grandmother Connie, her uncle Alex and all other members of her family, at this time there are no words adequate to express how we feel or our concern for you at this time of your loss. But we do open our hearts to you at this time, and from the bottom of our hearts, we do hug you and love you all.

Rachel's family has requested that this be an informal service and a time when we can gain insight as to how others remember Rachel, and also listen to some of the music that Rachel enjoyed.

 Rachel's father Robert and other family members and friends will now share with you their memories and thoughts and feelings about Rachel. We're going to play another song now, it's called 'Heal the World' by

Michael Jackson. After that Robert and others will say a few words."

I stood at the front of the Chapel at the Lectern and looked around the room. I could see the distraught faces of the family in front – Barb, Sharon, Alex, Judy, Wendy, Connie, Lorraine, and Paul. Rachel's close friends Kelly, Suzie, and Stacey, and her mother sat with the family.

My eyes swept mistily across those who had gathered there to pay their last respects to Rachel, and my heart filled with gratitude that so many had wanted to be there on the occasion.

The song ended. I had braced myself before speaking. (I thought, Rachel, this is for you.)

"The songs that we are playing today are some of Rachel's favourites, and I'm sure that she'd like to hear a bit more voice when the next one comes along, which is "Jesus Loves Me," so please join in."

I continued. (What follows are excerpts from what I said.)

"My daughter! Two small words that mean so much, that all the words ever written can't convey. Daughters bring so much richness, love, and beauty into all those lives they touch.

Rachel's life was very short but very sweet. And I guess that there are not many people who can say they lived their life without pain and sorrow, and Rachel can.

She was always loyal and would stand by you no matter what. She could not stand injustice in her short life. In any situation, if you had Rachel on your side, you were all right.

Rachel had empathy with all around her – with all living things – and with the earth. At any charity collection, Rachel would often make sure we made a donation, whether it was at a traffic light, or if someone came to the door. She had a passion for dolphins and sponsored one through the "Friends of Port Phillip Bay" organisation. This was a quality she shared with Sharon, who also sponsored a dolphin. Even though they were separate individuals they provided an inner strength for each other.

They shared a zest for life and experienced life to the full. They had plenty of adventure and had been to both the North and South Islands of New Zealand, and bonded with their extended family in England. She went to New Zealand again, alone this time, to visit her best friend Kelly and her family. Then we went to Sri Lanka excited and happy to see where her uncle and Dad had grown up. The holiday started with much happiness, but it was not meant to be.

During the last six months of her life, Rachel did a paper round and I drove her to do her deliveries. I didn't want her doing the rounds on her bike at that early hour of the morning on her own, so we loaded the papers into our Ford and she leaned out the window throwing the papers onto the drives as we went.

She had a keenly developed sense of fair play. A couple of months after she started her paper rounds she had the flu for a week, so I did the rounds for her. On Saturday morning, as usual, I drove her to the newsagent where she picked up her pay. When she got back into the car, she gave me the pay envelope. I said, "What's this?" She replied, "It's for you Dad, you did the rounds this week"

"Rachel," I said. "That's very sweet of you, but I did it for you. Keep it, love, it's for you." That was my Rachel.

After several weeks I thought I knew where which paper needed to be delivered to which house. I said to her, 'Rachel, as we go to each house I'm going to say 'Sun' or 'Age' and if I'm right you don't do anything, but if I'm wrong you whack me on the head with the rolled-up newspaper.'

We reached number five Wendy Court and I say, 'Sun' and the 'Sun' flies through the air and lands on the drive. Next one's the 'Age' and that's right. At number nine I say, 'Sun' and I feel a whack on my head. Made a mistake. This goes on for a while and then I say, 'Sun.'

Nothing happens. I wince, looks like I'm wrong.

"You winced, didn't you Dad?"

"Yes."

"Ha! I was tricking you, you were right!"

A ripple of laughter went through the Chapel.

"It is these happy memories of Rachel that we have to carry (my voice starts to break) to help us through our grieving, which is only natural. And I'm sure Rachel would want Sharon and all of us, once we have finished grieving for her, to take up that zest for life and go on living life to the full, knowing that she will always be with us in spirit, forever.

I am now going to call Rachel's three sisters, Sharon, Judy, and Wendy to come up and read a poem for Rachel."

They walked up, overcome with feeling, and shed a few tears, Sharon started the poem.

"Death is nothing at all

I have only slipped away into the next room

I am I, and you are you.

Whatever we were to each other that we still are.

Call me by my own familiar name,

Speak to me in the same easy way which we always used.

Put no difference in your tone,

Wear no air of sadness or sorrow.

Laugh, as we always laughed at the little jokes we enjoyed together."

Judy came in after a long deep sigh.

"Play. Smile, Think of me. Pray for me.

Let my name be the household word it always was.

Let it be spoken without an effort, without the ghost of a shadow in it."

(Her voice broke.)

"Let life mean all that it ever meant.

Why should I be out of your mind, because I'm out of your sight?"

Then it was Wendy's turn.

"I am waiting for you for an interval, somewhere very near,

Just around the corner.

All is well. Nothing is past – nothing is lost.

One brief moment and all will be as it was before."

One of Rachel's closest friends Suzie then spoke of her friendship with Rachel.

"Kelly and I have known Rachel basically all our lives, and even though it was a short life for Rachel, she did a lot of things for her age. Like visiting many countries.

She went rock climbing, she went to see the dolphins in the bay, and she adopted a dolphin –Nicky Finn, and she was always trying to find out more. If I wasn't going to Dolphin Meetings with her, she was writing away to find out more information so she could help save them. But I guess that's Rachel for you. Rachel and I were going to swim with the dolphins one day, and I know I will swim with them more than ever now, and when I do – Rachel will be there. She'll swim with me. Rachel was talented, kind, smart, and funny. She was pretty and she had a lot of things going for her, and all because she had such a loving and supporting family. Rachel was a perfect daughter, sister, grand-daughter, niece, and aunt, but most of all she was a perfect friend.

And I know most of you will agree. So what more could you ask for in a human being? Rachel, I'm not going to say goodbye. I'm just going to say thank you for blessing us all with your wisdom."

Poor Suzie broke down and sobbed, as I do now, as I recall the poignancy of these words all over again.

"Thank you, Suzie." In a voice that shook.

"Now here's Kelly, another very close friend, to recite a poem that she and Suzie composed about Rachel."

Kelly walked up to the front of the Chapel.

"Goodbye is such a permanent word,

Rachel won't leave, she just won't be heard.

Now as her body rests and her spirit runs free,

She can swim with the dolphins in the deep blue sea.

When the wind blows and the rain falls down,

 Rachel's there – she's all around.

The sun will rise to begin a new day,

 Rachel's there - smiling away!

Though goodbye is such a permanent word,

Rachel won't leave, she just won't be heard."

It was deeply moving.

I said, "I think it's all right to clap." There was a lot of released feeling as everyone clapped.

Then Stacey, another close friend of Rachel's, had a few words to say.

"Rachel, to me, was a very special person. She was an ambitious person, (Stacey was almost in tears, but bravely she continued) as well as intelligent, bright, funny, and understanding. Rachel was always there for me, whether in bad times or if I just needed a friend to go shopping with. She would also help me with my homework if I hadn't done it. Rachel showed me the different and ambitious side I had, that I didn't realise. She made me see that there was more to life than just sport – a career perhaps in Marine Biology, which we were both interested in. And now I will have to do it without her. But even if I don't succeed, Rachel will have given me the courage to try. And I'd like to read a short poem.

"To mourn too long for those we love is self-indulgent. But to honour their memory with a promise to live a little better for having known them gives purpose for their life and some reason for their death.

I'll never forget you, Rachel."

She just made it. Everyone clapped again and more tension was released.

Then came the song "Jesus loves me" by Whitney Houston.

Cliff took the lectern.

"Right, now I'm going to give a brief address. Then we're going to have a word of prayer for the family. After that we're going to commit her body into the hands of the Lord.

I've known Robert and Barbara for more than ten years. I'm not just here today as a Minister to take part in this funeral, but I've had the privilege of knowing the family for a long time. I've worked with Robert in a

Company. We used to work for the same Company together and that's where I got to know Robert.

As our friendship developed, I got to know Robert's family, and my wife and daughter, and Robert and his family used to spend a lot of time together. We came together for barbecues, and at Christmas time, birthdays and outings, and Evelyn and my daughter and myself, we counted it as a great privilege to have known this family. We got to know Mum Connie, and Alex as well, and it's always been good to know them.

We've had many occasions to enjoy the company of Rachel, and I remember them most especially at birthdays because Rachel would often come to my daughter's birthdays. It's at that time when children are playing together that you can kind of watch them and see what they are up to, and that way you can learn a lot about children. When they're together playing.

And one thing I'd tell you about Rachel that I noticed was that she was always smiling. You know that whenever Rachel came round she was never miserable

– she always had a smile on her face. She had that expression of joy and happiness. She always struck me as being a confident girl, and she had a very good attitude about her, you know she was always respectful, she had a lot of fairness, and she displayed this concern for others. These were some of the qualities that I noticed.

If the parties ran out of steam, it was always Rachel that got them stoked back up again. You know when things were quiet, she'd play a joke on somebody, she would do something and life would come back into the party.

Rachel also had beautiful expressive eyes. And from those eyes, you could see that she was very sensitive to the feelings of others.

We've heard today many things about Rachel, as people have talked about her, that have known her, and we have heard how Rachel was loyal and she stood by her friends – that's a very good quality. She stood by them no matter who they were, no matter what they had done, and no matter what others thought about them.

That is true friendship and I think we can all learn from her example in this.

We've heard about her compassion and her zest for life, and the world for Rachel was an exciting place.

We also know that each of us can be identified by our fingerprints. No two persons fingerprints are the same, we are told. Whatever we touch we leave behind our calling card. On whoever we meet we leave behind an impression, and Rachel left an impression on everyone she knew, and it was a positive one.

Everyone here today has happy and good feelings about Rachel. The things we've heard about Rachel today – we've heard about some of the things she has done. But rather it's been about Rachel, the person. Her personality and character today have come through loud and clear. I think when it boils down to it, we are remembered by our character, and the joy it brings to the lives of others.

In essence, Rachel was a unique person. The Bible tells us of another unique person who was loyal, compassionate, and forgiving, and his name was Jesus. He did not judge anyone. He did not condemn anyone, but He forgave everyone who asked Him, no matter who they were, no matter what they had done, and no matter what others thought of them. He recognises everyone's uniqueness and everyone's potential.

I've been asked to mention the fact that Rachel has now been set free, and indeed she has now been set free from this life to experience eternity.

So what is freedom? We think maybe of freedom of speech, freedom of choice, and freedom of passage. Some people have been denied all these freedoms, but have not regarded it as a restriction to their dreams and vision. Others have enjoyed all these freedoms but have been imprisoned in their minds by the bars of bitterness, un-forgiveness, and selfishness. Rachel was truly free in all respects – she didn't have any of these negative things about her personality.

Freedom is linked with right thinking, The Bible says that a person after death passes into eternity. The soul, which is composed of personality, character, and intelligence is indestructible. The hope we have is this, that because Jesus died in our place for our sins, so that we may all have eternal life if we believe in Him, that this will be so. The Bible teaches that death is a door through which we all pass.

You can break an appointment with your dentist, but you cannot miss your appointment with death. Rachel has left us in person, but she has left behind a message for each one of us, and that message is this, - to be loyal, compassionate, and forgiving, and to bring happiness into the lives of others, and in everything you do, do it honestly and completely. In essence, it's to love our neighbour as ourselves. For Jesus said such people inherit the Kingdom of Heaven.

We now come to the part of the service where I'd like you all to stand, please.

We are now going to commit the body of Rachel to God, and we know already that her spirit is gone through into eternity. Please close your eyes as I read this.

'For as much as it pleases Almighty God to take to Himself the soul of Rachel departed, we bear her body hence to the place prepared for it, that ashes may return to ashes, and dust to dust, and the imperishable spirit we find as by fire may be forever with the Lord.

And now may the Peace of God, which passeth all understanding, keep your hearts and minds, through Christ Jesus, and the Grace of the Lord Jesus Christ, and the Love of God and the Communion of the Holy Spirit be with you all, now and always. Amen.'

Whoever would like to now, may come down and pass by the coffin, if you wish. Also, the family have invited you all to their home if you would wish to afterwards, to some refreshments, and to join with them at this time. Thank you."

Then, as many of those gathered passed by Rachel's coffin for the last time, some of them placing a flower in remembrance, one of her favourite songs, "I'll Remember" by Madonna was being played. It was both sad and comforting. Some of us gathered outside as Rachel was taken away for her cremation. By arrangement, we had said goodbye in the Chapel, as we did not want to draw attention to the Cemetery Manager who was sticking his neck out for us. God Bless him.

"Goodbye my darling Rachel, - till we meet again." Our hearts were breaking as she was driven away. No words can describe what we were feeling. And yet, as people started to drift away and we moved to the car ourselves, Lorraine said, "I don't feel so bad now. That was a beautiful farewell."

Somehow, it gave us a lift. I felt our farewell to Rachel had been a "Celebration of her life."

These sentiments were echoed at home, where a houseful of family, friends, and neighbours gathered to give us their support. They helped with the preparation of platters of food, drink, and serving, and some stayed to help with the washing up. We had so many people to thank for standing by us at this time.

Finally, the last friend left, and after the remaining bits of tidying up, we sat down to a cup of tea with Lorraine and Kelly.

Later that night I lay in bed thinking of all the support we had that day, particularly the Cemetery Manager who went out on a limb for us. He didn't even know us. And all the family and friends who helped our flagging spirits. Everyone was concerned for Barb and me and how we were going to cope, and although they must have been concerned for how Sharon was feeling and would cope, no one thought to express those feelings to her. Someone said to her, "You must be strong for Mum." Really? It's all very well showing concern for Mum and Dad, she thought, 'but what about me?'

She had lost her little sister, for God's sake! There would be a big struggle for her to endure. For all of us. But particularly for her.

It was going to be a long hard road ahead of us. Long and winding. There were stages of grieving to go through and months of hurting.

We were not looking forward to it.

We hardly slept a wink that night.

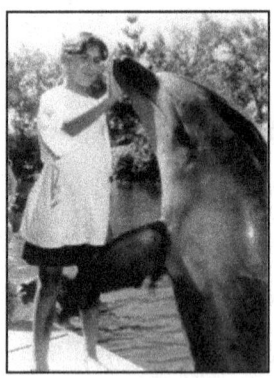

Chapter Thirty Seven

I woke with a start the next morning, after a fitful sleep. It was 4.15 a.m. the time I usually woke for the paper round with Rachel. From our bedroom we could see into the room Sharon shared with Rachel - the doors were at right angles to our bedroom. I could see Rachel's bed. I looked over with a feeling of physical pain in my chest, a sudden fear.

My God! Rachel's not there. She will never be there again! Fear gripped me as I thought, 'How are we going to do this? How are we all going to continue with our lives?'

She was so much a part of our lives, which were focussed around seeing Sharon and Rachel growing up, being part of that growth, from children into young women. Watching them make their choices, helping them with their school work, seeing them make new friends, and watching over their relationships. Nurturing them, loving them, supporting them. Encouraging them in the sports they participated in, like Netball on Saturdays. It was the natural order of things.

No more.

Now it was Sharon on her own. But Sharon was herself now half of a pair of sisters. Suddenly thrust into premature adulthood, or so it seemed. How will she handle the pressure?

'Would Mum and Dad now become stiflingly overprotective?'

And Barb? If Sharon withdraws into herself, would it mean that she has lost not one but two daughters? How does Barb relate to Sharon and me? All these questions.

I look around the room. Usually, by now Rachel is at the window seat waiting for me to slip on my sweats and runners, so we can be first in line for the papers.

What is going on? What has happened to our normal, happy, peaceful life?

It was just too good to last. Barb said that she had had the same feeling, and had started to 'pay her dues' – donating to several charities, so we could keep the 'status quo'. Then she said, about six months before, she had a dream that Rachel was killed in an accident. She spent many nights watching over her as she slept. Why didn't she tell us? She didn't want us to worry.

An overwhelming feeling of sadness and fear overcame me as I prepared to face another lonely day. This was how it was for all of us for months. And somehow we had to keep going. We had no alternative, even if it felt like we were in an inescapable trap.

We needed an escape. Somewhere to lick our wounds and ground ourselves to face the future. Wendy had returned to the Gold Coast, and Lorraine and Kelly went back home to New Zealand. Connie had settled into life after Rachel.

Judy, Paul, Sharon, Alex, Barb, and I drove up into the mountains for a short break. We booked a lodge at Mt. Buller and settled in when we got there on a Saturday afternoon. We decided we'd tire ourselves out with a bushwalk. That was partly successful. That night Alex had a dream about Rachel. She walked into the lounge, in the lodge and he said, "Rachel, what are you doing here? You're not supposed to be here."

Rachel replied, "You can see me, but you can't touch me." He extended his hand and the dream ended.

We stayed indoors a lot, and one afternoon Judy, Paul, and Sharon went on a trail ride. Rachel loved horses and trail rides.

On the way back home, Barb, Sharon, and Judy noticed an advertisement for Joy rides in a light plane, so we stopped and booked a flight.

"We've got to do *something,*" they said. "Don't you want to come?"

"I think I'll sit this one out," I said. I wasn't feeling up to it. We watched them take off, and I started to get nervous. The ride seemed to take forever. I paced in front of the booking office. "I hope they're okay," I said.

"They'll be fine," said Barb. "Stop worrying." But I was on tenterhooks till they got back safely. Then it was back home to pick up the threads of life again.

Barb engrossed herself into writing a journal, Sharon kept to her room listening to music and writing, coping as best she could.

Barb was over-protective of Sharon, which Sharon found stifling. I just listened, when she wanted to talk, and that was what she needed.

The relationship between mother and daughter became strained. It was sad. Sharon seemed to relate to me because I was just 'there' for her, I guess.

We went through all the stages of grief – denial, anger, bargaining, depression, and acceptance. It wasn't easy, but it was inevitable.

I read books, one after the other, "Why Bad Things Happen to Good People", "Past Lives Present Dreams", "The Road Less Travelled", "Why Me, Why This?", "God in Us".

It was three weeks before I went back to work. When I did, I did what Judy had done when she went back to work at the hospital where she worked as a Physiotherapist. I gathered the staff in the cafeteria and said to them, "I know it's going to be awkward. Most of you may not know what to say to me, or how to treat me. But let me tell you what happened. It may make it easier for all of us."

They listened in silence as I related to them what had happened in Sri Lanka, and I thanked them for all their love and support. "Please don't ignore me, or look the other way when we cross in a corridor or wherever. Just treat me normally." Slowly the awkwardness passed.

I remember crossing the street outside my office to the Café across the road to get a sandwich and a coffee and seeing a truck coming towards me on the street. I thought to myself. 'Take me, but take me quickly.' And then I realised that was selfish because there were people who needed me.

It was time to get back on track.

We grieved in our way and as the months passed, we gradually found our way back. Barbara was engrossed in her work and found an outlet in art. She painted in oils and water-colour and had entered her work in exhibitions and even won prizes, and had special mentions in the galleries in which she exhibited. She even put on an exhibition and was successful in selling her work.

Sharon moved out to live with her boyfriend and his mother who ran a Fairy Shop, and she conducted Story Telling sessions with kids in the shop. She struggled with her grief over an extended time and it was years before she was back to normal.

I buried myself in my work to the exclusion of everything else, and it was that focus that kept me going. For relaxation, I played golf every weekend with Alex and friends.

Time passed.

Time heals.

And it did, eventually.

Chapter Thirty Eight
Dreams and recollections

Friday 13 January 1995

It was after dinner, and we were sitting around the dining table talking about things we had to do. Barb left the table and went to the bedroom. Sharon, Rachel, and I decided to go into the sitting room. Just as we passed the window I hugged Rachel and thought how *real* she was. I hugged her tighter and felt her weight and thought she was getting heavy, as I carried her through the kitchen. I suddenly thought . . . she's not gone she is *here!*

I was excited. Happy even.

But as we walked further into the kitchen she seemed to gradually go lighter in my arms and seemed to grow smaller gradually, and I thought, 'Oh well, she's not here after all.' But then life seemed to come back into her body and she said, "Carry me, Dad."

"I am."

"Take me back to the dining room," and I walked back with her in my arms to the dining room . . .

Sunday 15 January 1995

Last evening, during my walk I had an imaginary conversation with Rachel telling her about what was happening at work, and that I loved her and missed her. She seemed to say, "I know, Dad. But I'm always here over your shoulder."

"Thanks, Rachel. Remember all these houses on our paper round? I miss you most on those paper rounds."

"I know."

"Remember that park over there and how I used to chase you and Sharon around the play equipment?"

"Yep," Then she said, "I've got to go, but I'll always be around you."

I said, "Okay love, thanks." I walked on with tears in my eyes.

I felt her say, "Now Dad, you shouldn't be doing that."

I said, "Sorry. I'll be okay, Rache." And I felt her leave. And felt a sense of comfort.

Late January

"Take me away, Rachel."

"I can't. Your time has not yet come."

"How come your time came before mine?"

"I don't know. I had nothing to do with that."

Standing at the pier at Rosebud, watching the sun go down over the horizon, composing a poem.

A bud that never opened

A flower that never bloomed,

A love that never faltered,

Done too soon.

Then more.

A heart that's crushed and twisted,

A load too hard to bear,

A sea of tears growing larger.

An ache too mine to share.

The sun rises on a crisp spring morning

Over the distant hills,

As I stand on the pier at Rosebud

Missing Rachel.

Another dream.

Standing in a field of flowers, sensing the presence of others but seeing no one.

"What do I have to do before . . . ?"

"Before you move on there's a deal of healing to be done."

"How do I know what to do? I'm not qualified to do this."

"Don't worry, it will come to you. We will help you."

Rachel, in another dream . . .

"Before we can all be together again, there are four things that have to be done, and I have done one."

Chapter Thirty Nine

There were three distinct phases in my healing. The first was the awakening of my spirituality. I was visiting my daughter Wendy in Queensland when one day she said to me. "Dad, you've been having migraines for years, and I know someone who may be able to help you. My friend Anya – she's from Sweden. She practices a modality called 'Body Harmony' and I think you should go see her."

I agreed, and she set up an appointment for me.

To see Anya, I had to drive a few kilometres up in the mountains of Queensland right on the border of New South Wales. Anya and her husband Brendan lived in a country style house up a steep drive.

Anya was tall, beautiful, with blonde hair and keen sparkling eyes. She greeted me with a smile. "Hi, you must be Robert. Wendy just called to say you were on the way. Please come in." As we walked to her consulting room she said, "How can I help you?"

I replied, "Well, Wendy said you would be able to help me with my migraines, but what's worrying me right now is the grief over my daughter's death."

She led me to her massage table and motioned for me to lie on it. "Let's see what we can do," she said.

I lay face up, and she stood at the head of the table and placed her hands under my head. I looked up at the ceiling. She said nothing. I lay there for a while wondering what was coming next. She remained silent. I closed my eyes. After a long while of silence, I felt a twitching in my chest. Then my chest heaved involuntarily. I felt more twitches in my chest and wondered what was going on. Anya still stayed silent. After a long while, I sighed, and a feeling of calmness came over me. I opened my eyes and said, "What was that?"

"Probably some emotion getting away." Then she moved to the side of the bed, on my right, and said. "Now let's do some circular breathing, do you know how to do this?"

"No," I replied, "I don't."

"Don't worry, I'll help you. Breathe in and out rapidly, don't pause your breath. Do it with me," she said and did as she had explained. I followed her. Anya had one hand under my back and her palm on my chest.

In a short while, I felt my chest swell with emotion, as I continued breathing in this way, and then suddenly I felt myself sobbing uncontrollably. I sobbed, and sobbed, my breath catching, tears streaming down my face, till I felt completely spent and exhausted. Anya, with her hand still on my chest, encouraged me. "You're doing well. Let it out. Just let it all come out. That's right, keep letting it all come out." I lay there, not moving. Just 'being'.

A sense of calm came over me that I hadn't felt in a long while. I felt at peace, and as if I'd lost a heavy weight off my shoulders. I sighed deeply. Then I said, "I feel so at peace now in my chest, but you know I feel a lot of tension in my legs."

"I know," she said, "Let's work on that."

With that, she stood at the foot of the massage table and placed her hands der the calves of my legs. Once again she said nothing, just stood there, calmly. Then an amazing feeling came over me. I could *feel* the tension leaving my legs, going up and out. It was something I had never experienced before. I sighed again as I lay there, calm, peaceful, and relaxed. I had let a lot of pent up emotion leave my body (and mind) and felt so much at peace.

Anya smiled at me. "How do you feel now?" she asked.

"I feel so calm," I said, "That was awesome. I've never experienced anything like this before. What did you do?"

She said, "I was just *there* for you."

It was a new experience for me. I said, "I don't understand how you did that, but you don't know just how much you have helped me, and what it means to me. Thank you so much."

She hugged me and said, "You take care now, Robert." I left, feeling a sense of relief, and more relaxed than I had been for months

Chapter Forty

The next phase in my healing was the continuation of my spiritual awakening, this time through the healing power of therapeutic massage. For a whole year, on Saturday mornings, my good friend and masseuse Katelyn massaged the kinks out of my neck, shoulders, and back.

There was more to it than that, though.

I had done a lot of reading about a modality called Body Harmony. It is believed that from the time you are very little, any traumatic experiences that are too difficult for your mind to deal with manifest themselves in the tissues of your body, as knots in your muscles. It is only when issues are resolved sub-consciously that these can be released emotionally and physically.

As Katelyn worked tirelessly, I could feel her tease out the tight knots in me as she pressed and released, and as this process went on a feeling of calmness and relaxation followed. Massages which were scheduled to last for an hour never stopped this side of two, and as the weeks turned into months, an emotional change occurred that was deeply spiritual. I can only explain it by saying that a new awakening occurred within me and, as time went on, I felt an increasing sense of peacefulness and a love for everyone and everything. There's no other way of expressing my experience.

After each massage, Katelyn would sit at the foot of the massage table and hold my feet in her hands wordlessly. I could literally feel the energy from her hands enter my feet and circle back through her hands again. This was something I had never experienced before and I realised I was becoming more in tune with my inner self, both emotionally and physically. It was deeply healing. And if there was anything positive to be gained from my loss, this inner peace was a manifestation of my recovery that I couldn't have anticipated. I will always be grateful to Katelyn for the part she so caringly played in this phase of my spiritual growth.

Chapter Forty One

I began to question my purpose for being on this planet and what I should do for the rest of my time. I felt an increasing desire to be of use to others to justify my being here. If I could be of help to others it would make sense in my life.

I found myself being led to the next phase of my recovery through hypnotherapy. I cannot remember what precipitated my interest in it, but I read an article on hypnotism and was instantly captivated by its capacity to help others. I read again, that traumatic experiences in early life could be dropped into one's subconscious, bypassing the usual filter of conscious analysis, and affect one for years.

For instance, when very young, if a father told his kid, "You are the most disobedient kid in the street. I can't get you to do anything I ask," the kid would believe that he was 'the most disobedient kid on the street.' This would lodge in his subconscious, and when asked to do something his subconscious mind would remind him that he was disobedient, because that was what he believed. That behaviour would be reinforced. Any incident that triggered that memory in the future would elicit that same response,

You can't blame problem children for their behaviour.

The opposite is also true if a child was told, "You are an amazing kid, and can do anything you put your mind to. I am so proud of you." High achievers have a lot to thank their parents for.

I completed a course in hypnotherapy and was able to help people with issues they had, like giving up smoking, losing weight, increasing self-esteem, and overcoming phobias. It helped my self-esteem that I could contribute to others' progress.

One interesting case history comes to mind of a Senior Executive in an International Company who came to see me because he was afraid to fall asleep. When he felt he was dozing off he would shake himself awake. He didn't want to fall asleep. This affected him in phases throughout his life. He was then in his fifties.

I relaxed him with a sensitive induction and regressed him back to a time when something traumatic would have happened to him that precipitated this fear of falling asleep.

He was deeply relaxed in a trance and I said, "Now let your mind go back, way back in time when this became a problem for you, you won't have to do anything. Just relax and let your mind wander, and travel back, way, way back. And when you get to that point, just nod your head to let me know you are there."

There was silence for a while and then I saw a slight nod of his head.

"That's very good," I said. "Now tell me how old you are and where you are."

He said he was six years old and in his parents' bedroom. He'd had a nightmare and wanted to get into bed with his parents. But his father said he was a strong little boy and should learn to sleep in his bed in his room. So he had to go back to his bed but did not want to fall asleep because he didn't want to have another nightmare.

This had affected him all through his life and there were phases where he just did not want to fall asleep.

By re-visiting the time and the experience, and processing it in his mind, and realising that he did not need to react to that memory the way he had been doing, helped him to overcome his fear of falling asleep.

My experiences with hypnotherapy were all part of my healing.

Chapter Forty Two

As time went on Barb and I tended to go our own way. Barb was engrossed in her work and her painting. She had a circle of friends in the Arts Society to which she belonged, and spent a lot of time with them.

I was absorbed in my work and golf on weekends. We were never able to grieve together. They say that eighty percent of marriages in which a child is lost don't survive, but I thought that ours belonged to the twenty percent that did. But it was not to be.

We gradually drifted apart.

One June, at a Mind Body and Spirit Festival in Melbourne I sponsored a Hypnotherapy Stall at which we introduced people to its healing power. Across from my stall was a stall promoting "Dominant" household cleaning products. I walked across and got talking to the stallholders, and that was where I met Jan.

Jan was bubbly and energetic with sparkling blue eyes, and I was attracted to her. We shared a coffee in the Exhibition cafeteria while we chatted, and formed a friendship that grew beyond the Exhibition and the weekend.

We kept in touch and I learned that both our marriages were on rocky ground.

When the split occurred in both our marriages, Jan and I moved in together and we have been together since. After buying a house together, I decided to pop the question.

We were at a New Year's Eve Dance with our friends Robbie and Maggie. After the main meal, I made as if I was going to the restroom and when I was out of sight of our table, I made my way towards the kitchen and found the waitress who was serving at our table.

"Hi," I said, "Would you mind doing me a favour?"

"What can I do for you?" She asked.

"We're having Crème Brulee for dessert," I said and gave her the engagement ring I had bought for Jan. "Would you mind popping this ring in the bowl you place next to mine, on my left?"

"Oh!" she squealed. "A proposal! How romantic. I'd be glad to do that for you."

When Jan noticed the ring on top of her Crème Brulee, to say she was surprised would be an understatement. She took a minute to get over her surprise, but she said yes.

We were married in Basterfield Park in Moorabbin on a sunny winter's morning and held a Reception at a nearby elegant Reception Hall.

During the speeches, my daughter Judy said, "When Dad met Jan she put the spark that was missing back into his life."

She did. And it hasn't gone out. Thank you, Jan.

We travelled to England and Europe on our honeymoon and Jan met the English side of my family. Trips to Egypt and Greece followed as we both have a love of travel. Jan has a bubbly personality, a love of animals, is fiercely loyal and has a keen sense of fair play. Jan is the most generous person I know and is always there to help those in need. She has helped a needy family in Nepal and elsewhere. I was keen to take her to Sri Lanka.

Chapter Forty Three

Taking Jan back to the land of my birth.

A time to remember

It was a journey back in time, a time when a journey was an adventure. Of youth, of growth, of wonder and excitement, a time never to be forgotten. And so it was that in May 2014, I took Jan back to the land of my birth, where my life was shaped, where I went to school, grew up, and became who I am. It was my Sri Lanka, or Ceylon as I knew it for most of my life there.

We touched down at Colombo International Airport at midnight and stepped out into the warm humid air that I remember so well. I felt I was going home.

The airport was crowded for that time of night with travellers scampering for their transport, and we scoured the arrival area for the Jetwing rep. There he was holding up the name board, upside down. One look at his twinkling eyes and cheeky look and we knew we would hit it off with Anton. We drove down to the Jetwing Beach Hotel Negombo, where we were booked into an impressive room overlooking the beach. This was the start of an awesome two weeks.

The next morning at the restaurant serving breakfast, which looked out right onto the beach, we feasted on paw-paws, avocado drinks, egg-hoppers, and good old Ceylon tea. Just outside on the beach, squirrels scampered across the sand and scuttled up the coconut palms lining the way to the ocean. Jan could hardly wait to go out and make their acquaintance, as they fed from her hand before she dipped her feet in the Indian Ocean.

Then it was off driving through the not forgotten streets of Negombo, past the now walled premises of Newstead Girls' School, where Mum was Matron of the hostel.

We arrived at the Pinnawala Elephant Orphanage where young elephants left behind by their herd or strayed away from it, are cared for and nurtured. It was wonderful to walk amongst them as they wound their way down the streets of Pinnawala, up close and personal, to the river where they frolicked and enjoyed their daily river bath. Their keepers, or mahouts, kept a watchful eye on them.

A long drive through the south-central part of the island followed before we reached Kandalama, our base for the next three nights. Here we stayed at the Heritance Hotel – a five-star hotel that doesn't just sit on the landscape but is part of it. For instance, floor to ceiling windows on the far side of the Jacuzzi in the bathroom looked straight out onto jungle vines on which monkeys clambered and birds perched in all their colourful splendour.

After dinner and restful sleep, I woke the next morning to a long-forgotten birdsong…the instantly familiar 'kok-korr' (pause)… 'kok-korr' … (another pause)…

'kok-korr'. It was the cry of the Sri Lankan yellow fronted barbet. (Close your eyes and listen, - can't you almost hear it?) Smiling I stretched, rose from my bed, and walked out onto the balcony in my boxer shorts. Overlooking the treetops of the jungle, stretching for miles in front of me, in the hazy morning light, was the silhouette of Sigiriya, the ancient rock castle of King Kasyapa rising out of the distant plain.

Birds tweeted and chirped around me, waiting for the sun, hidden behind a distant hill, to peep out from behind it and kiss the verdant treetops, bathing them in the glow of a vibrant sunrise, lazily announcing the start of another day in a jungle paradise.

Childhood memories of similar mornings came flooding back as I stood on the balcony in my sentimental reverie.

We were advised to keep our balcony doors closed at all times, but after I had taken some pictures of the sunrise, I had left them open as I walked back into the room to get my ipad.

When I turned around I was surprised to see a monkey in the room. It was a kind of khaki coloured rhesus, with a pink face, inquisitive eyes, lean body, gangly limbs, and long tail. He went straight for the tray with the tea and sugar and grabbed a handful of sugar sachets. He knew what he was doing, and made for the door. In his haste he found himself caught up in the curtains trying to find his way to the glass door.

I moved towards him trying to shepherd him towards the door, but he came out from behind the curtains near the wall and made his way towards the front of the room, towards the bed, where Jan was just waking up. I said, "There's a monkey in the room. He's taken something!"

Jan sat up in alarm thinking of her diabetes meds and got up from the bed. The monkey was just a few feet away from her and she made a shooing motion with her hands to guide him towards the window. This made him feel threatened and he grimaced, snarled, leaped in the air, and struck out at Jan's face giving her a superficial scratch just above her lip. In a move to protect herself, she fell to the floor, face down, and I moved between her and the monkey, with my computer case in front of me, so he had no option but to move towards the window, and out onto the balcony. I quickly shut the door and checked on Jan.

The scratch was superficial and there was a red line where his claws had struck her, but it was not bleeding. She applied some alcohol, as we reviewed the start to our second morning of the trip.

The staff at breakfast showed real concern over the scratch, and by the time we went down to the reception area to meet Anton for the day's events, word had got around and the Management insisted that Anton take us down to the Hotel doctor.

At the clinic, the doctor saw us instantly despite having another patient, a young lady, in his consulting room. The patient didn't seem to mind and was concerned about the scratch. We were advised that it was best to get a course of anti-rabies injections, as a precaution, so we went to the nearest hospital. Here we were taken straight to the head of the 30 long queue and after formalities, to the head of the queue waiting at the injection room. No one seemed to mind, showing concern for the monkey scratch. We were in an out in a matter of minutes.

We climbed Sigiriya next, stopping halfway up the 200- metre ancient rock citadel to view the amazing 1500-year old frescoes painted in a rock cave. When Jan made it to the Lions' Paw staircase just below the summit, I thought she had done well, but on she went, up the steep ascent to the summit. She was determined and completed the more than 1200 steps in all, to the top where we viewed the ruins of the castle and gardens of King Kasyapa who ruled the area some 1500 years ago.

We stood atop the ruins of the ancient castle at the summit of the rock monolith, envisioning the scene as it would have been ....the impressive palace building, the surrounding gardens, and crops being grown. The hustle and bustle of daily life as the King and his courtiers, clad in traditional colourful dress, carried out their duties, damsels frolicking in the palace baths. We imagined the sentries atop the citadel scouring the countryside far and wide, all around, on alert for any sign of the king's brother, Moggollana, the rightful heir to the throne. (Kasyapa was the favoured but illegitimate son of King Dhatusena and had assumed the throne on his father's death.)

Then the arrival of Mogggollana with a large army, ready to do battle with Kasyapa, at the head of his, as the brothers approached each other on elephants. Kasyapa's elephant hesitating, because the ground was soft underfoot, and turning to take a firmer route, taking his master into battle with his brother.

Kasyapa's army, thinking the detour of the elephant meant that he was retreating, causing them to abandon the battle against a far superior army, and disband in disarray. Kasyapa, seeing his army desert him, knowing this was the end, taking out his dagger and taking his own life. Moggollana seeing his dead brother, and assuming his Kingship, cremating Kasyapa and leaving the site, never to return.

The poet John Still describes it thus:

"From his belt, he drew a dagger forth

And plunged it fiercely deep into his throat.

Slowly he sank upon the elephant

Bowing his head upon its reeking neck

And so he died, unconquered to the end."

We brought our thoughts back to the present. It was hot work, we were dripping with sweat, feeling perspiration dribbling down our backs, as we made our way down to the base, and back to reality.

That night, after a sumptuous dinner in the restaurant it was a complete surprise when members of the restaurant staff came out singing, 'Happy Birthday' to the strains of a violin with a lighted birthday cake. It was very touching and I had a picture taken with the staff and the cute chef who made the cake.

Jan had asked me how to greet people in Sinhalese and when I told her "Ayubowan" and we greeted people, the reaction was spontaneous and welcoming. When I was able to talk in Sinhalese the staff's eyes lit up and I was made to feel so welcome. It was amazing. They seemed proud that I remembered, and that I still identified with my Sri Lankan heritage. They mentioned that so many seemed to forget when they left, and I think that's sad. I am proud of my heritage, and always will be.

The more I talked the more I remembered, and they thought I was quite fluent. The Sinhalese are such genuine caring people, and the feeling of open-heartedness was mutual and I count myself so lucky to have grown up in that culture.

The next day we visited Polonnaruwa, another ancient capital, and walked amongst the ruins of the city with its audience halls, dagobas, and giant statues of the Buddha carved out of rock in a famous rock temple.

After a stopover at the Dambulla rock caves, which were colourful and interesting, we made our way past Matale to my old home town Kandy.

It was Wesak, the celebration of the May full moon, and one of the customs of the Buddhists is that people take up a collection and put up a roadside stall and provide short eats for anyone who cares to stop by, and this is free of charge.

These stalls line the streets at intervals and passers-by, are waved in to join in a bite and a chat. This is open to anyone, and is called "Dansala."

We were passing a stall run by the local Police and Anton pulled over so we could partake of their hospitality. As Anton said, "This is probably the only time when we get anything from the cops, other than something like a speeding ticket."

We joined the cops in a feed of hot boiled chickpeas, served in muslin bags. They posed for a picture and I found myself surrounded by cops, chatting to them in Sinhalese. I told them about my Sri Lankan roots and of how I had left the island all those years ago

We drove on to Kandy, home of my youth, where I went to school and was raised, - the platform for my adult life. It was like re-visiting my youth again.

We went around to all my old haunts, looking for the places where we lived, the cinemas we went to, the lake we sailed as boy scouts while in school, the mountains we climbed, my old school, our sister school, Girls High School – the scene of many a teenage romance, the botanical gardens, where we went with our butterfly nets adding to our collection of butterflies. Memories came flooding back, and for a while, I was a boy again.

We strolled down the well-remembered pathways in the botanical gardens that evening, one of them flanked by yellow and red foliage, still a feature after all these years. Memories of chasing rare and colourful species of butterflies in this very place brought a nostalgic smile to my face.

Birds chirped in the trees, and a black and yellow birdwing butterfly flitted across the path to settle on a blue flower. Brilliant red salvia, and coxcomb, orange and yellow flowers of different species spread out all around us as we walked, and then the tall avenue of palms came into view, as local couples, and families strolled along, enjoying the walk.

As we crossed we exchanged smiles. Smiles that came from the eyes, genuine and warm. An unspoken communication seemed to take place. A communication that seemed to say, "We acknowledge your greeting, and we welcome your greeting, - and it feels good." I felt welcome, as did Jan, and I felt I was home. It was an amazing feeling and I remember thinking – it doesn't get much better than this.

Jan mentioned on one occasion, "They're smiling at you. It's the girls!" I chuckled. After all those years, going back to the scenes of my youth like this – I felt I was a part of it all.

The next morning we drove down Lady Blake's Drive alongside the Mahaweli River, and I remembered sitting on the bar of a bicycle ridden by my Dad on that stretch of road before he left to join the British Army during the World War 2.

On an embankment just below the road, a traditional Kandyan wedding was commencing with the wedding party in full traditional dress. Jan was eager to take pictures and Anton stopped the car, went down the steps to where it was all happening, and spoke to someone in the party.

He then came back up and told us it would be fine to go down and take a few pictures. We scurried down the steps and were surprised when people in the wedding party invited us to take as many pictures as we wanted and even directed us to where the bride was getting ready and said she would pose for Jan. They even asked us to stay and join in the celebration. We thanked them but did not stay. We had a full day ahead of us.

That evening we attended a cultural show with Kandyan Dancing in full regalia, and many male and female traditional dances, and were treated to the throbbing beat of traditional drums,

The smiles and the looks of the performers were so expressive and seemed to say, "This is us. This is what we do, and we love sharing it with you." The audience was mainly foreign tourists.

The next morning I visited my old school, Kingswood College. I got talking to some staff members in Sinhalese, recounting my time as a student. Seeing again the senior school, the school hall (scene of many a school concert) the smelly chemistry lab, and the Primary block. I met the Principal, at his residence where we once lived when my uncle was School Principal.

The old school bell was still there, still doing its job some 57 years since I left.

I glanced up at the College building and could see the door to what was the English Literature Class. I could see myself walking up to it, turning the handle and entering, - looking around the class to find my seat, scraping my chair on the concrete floor, sitting down. Looking up at the blackboard and seeing what Mr. Abeyratne had scrawled in white chalk across the top.

"Students, like pins, are useless when they lose their heads." He would walk into class and write a quotation before each lesson, and not say a word, It was up to us his students to write them down to remember, or not.

I have a long list of quotations in my notebook. "Errors, like straws, upon the surface float. Ye who seek pearls must dive below,"

"A thing of beauty is a joy forever." There were more.

Then it was up to the high country, to the mountains covered by nothing other than tea bushes and shade trees. High up in tea country we visited a tea plantation, Mackwoods, and saw how tea manufactured, plucked, dried, fermented, rolled, tasted, graded, and packed for despatch. Of course, we got to sample a 'cuppa' in the cafeteria. You could smell the fragrance of fresh tea.

Nuwara Eliya (known as 'Little England') was not how I remembered it. But then again most of the cities weren't. They had become crowded and untidy over the years. But I chose to remember them as they were.

Anton took us through the market, lined with colourful fruit and vegetable stalls,

In Nuwara Eliya we stayed at the Heritance, a tea factory converted into a hotel, before traveling to Bandarawela two and a half hours away, where we visited my niece Susan and her husband Gerald. It was wonderful to see her and her children. Jan was welcomed with open arms and had found a new family.

Susan has a beautiful property called Seven Springs with a lush tropical garden filled with colourful flowers like caladium, bleeding heart, roses, and cosmos. Fruit trees like pawpaw and banana line the perimeter.

The Sri Lankan way of calling people 'uncle' and 'auntie' touched Jan and she 'inherited' many new nieces and nephews.

After a sumptuous lunch of curry and rice, we drove down to Ella, and a resort called '98 Acres' comprising twelve eco-lodges set on a tea plantation. The lodge we occupied, with a thatched roof and an open outlook, commanded sweeping views of the surrounding plantations amongst mountains on all sides. It was an idyllic setting. We had to walk through tea bushes, and up a few steps to the open restaurant, past an inviting swimming pool.

The next day we drove down to sea level again to Yala on the south coast, the location of Yala National Park or wild-life sanctuary. The Jetwing Hotel Yala sits directly adjacent to the beach, and after settling in and showering, it was time for our first Safari.

We climbed aboard the safari jeep with cameras at the ready, and after entering the park and passing a few rather friendly wild elephants, the excitement grew when we saw a group of other jeeps stopped on the sandy road, with all aboard peering intently into the jungle trees.

They were looking for a leopard, and we stopped alongside them and peered intently into the trees… and there it was! A majestic looking leopard, draped lazily over a branch amongst the foliage, tail flicking from side to side, like a giant cat.

We saw wild buffalo, elephants, (one very obviously pregnant) a Sri Lankan bear, wild boar, deer, and a large variety of birds like peacocks, kingfishers, and other colourful winged wonders. And crocodiles, stalking herons in a pool.

We saw where the tsunami of December 2004 had roared in with giant rolling waves, destroying homes, lives, and wild-life too, causing so much death and devastation.

In the hotel restaurant next morning at breakfast, Jan wanted more milk in her tea and the waiter obliged her willingly, topping up her cup. I nonchalantly said in Sinhalese, "Thava tikak tharnna" (Pour a bit more). He was so surprised to hear me speak in Sinhalese, he looked at me, stunned, pouring milk all over the table cloth. I just chuckled wickedly.

The ride from Yala to Ahungulla was uneventful as we traversed the south-west coast of the island, pausing at a wayside fruit stall for Jan to experience her first taste of a king coconut drink, A quick tour of an old Dutch Fort at Galle followed.

The Heritance at Ahungalla was yet another hotel set right on the beach, where the food and service were excellent as always, and we were graced with a spectacular sunset.

Once again there were signs of the catastrophic tsunami of 2004, with several memorials and humble grave sites lining the roadside. Anton recounted how the Galle Express had been engulfed by a giant wave on its journey, swamped off its tracks in a seemingly disdainful show of the power of the ocean, twisting the mighty metal monster as it rolled and twisted its way across the coastal countryside killing all on board.

We met up with my sister Barbara and her family, my nieces, their husbands, and children, and more, and the Sri Lankan side of Jan's new family had swelled in numbers.

The way they embraced Jan into the fold, and how Jan received their acceptance was heart-warming and emotional, and Jan had fallen in love, not only with Sri Lanka but with her expanding new family as well.

We then witnessed a remarkable feat. My grand-nephew Jason was able to read with his eyes closed. Yes, right, with his eyes closed! When his father Joe, told us about this ability, Jason was all embarrassed and shy. Jason was 13 years old. His math teacher had recognized some special ability he had and introduced him to a teacher from New Zealand who was at his school and was able to teach him to use his mid-brain.

It is said that this can be taught to children up to the ages of about thirteen.

Jan was asked to choose a book, and any passage at random from the book, while Jason was blindfolded. Not only with a handkerchief, but with Jan's scarf as well bound tightly across his face. Jan then gave the book to Joe, who held it upside down on Jason's lap.

Jason began to read, word for word, what was on the page in front of him. He read slowly, sometimes pausing between words, but they were exactly what was in the book. There were two pictures on the opened pages and Joe asked, "Can you describe the pictures?"

Jason replied, "There are two walls, running parallel, and a woman standing between them." Exactly as it was in the book. Then he described the other picture too. I captured it all on video. It was amazing to watch.

Jason was humble and shy about his ability. When we asked him how he did it, he answered that he was able to, 'see it, like it was on a screen'.

When Anton told his brother about it, his brother had replied, "He must have memorized the book". This doesn't hold water because he didn't know which book Jan had chosen, nor what page it was opened to before he was asked to read.

We spent the night at the Mount Lavinia hotel, and the next day we visited the Colombo Zoo in sweltering heat – and this was a disappointment. The Zoo, which we remembered so well, was looking tired and untidy - we felt it was uncared for and the animals like the 'big four' looked bored and unhappy. The cruelty of keeping these once magnificent beasts caged and closely confined hit home hard. It was not a pleasant memory.

We drove around Colombo, visiting old haunts, places where I had lived, streets I had wandered in my youth, suburbs we frequented, and some of it again looked tired and untidy. There was a lot of construction work going on and this did not help the impression of

Colombo. There were no privacy screens like we see at home on construction sites.

I chose to remember it as it was when I lived there, just a normal city with its usual hustle and bustle.

We spent our last night at the Cinnamon Grand and visited my cousin Astrid the next day, which we spent relaxing.

Anton joined us for dinner that night before driving us along the newly constructed highway to the place where this two-week spectacular holiday had begun, at the airport, before we bade him a fond farewell and boarded our 1.30 a.m. flight back home.

It was indeed a time to remember, not only what was, but what is – on our sentimental journey back in time. It was a wonderful holiday one which neither Jan nor I would ever forget. I was happy that I was able to introduce Jan to my Sri Lanka for her to see for herself the culture in which I was raised. We were able to connect with the heart and soul of Sri Lanka, the people who lived away from the city and, truly feel the heartbeat of the gentle people of this jewel of an island.

The fact that she fell in love with the land, the people, and the new (expanding) side of my family was indeed the icing on the cake.

Chapter Forty Four

We were back again for Christmas with the Sri Lankan side of the family. They were as happy to share Christmas with us as we were to share it with them.

Jan is very much a 'Christmas' person and we always decorate our front window for the season with a different theme each year. The garden is filled with Christmas lights and outdoor decorations. Jan takes delight in watching the looks on children's faces as they walk down the street and stop to look in at our window.

"Look, Mum, It's Santa Claus in the chimney."

"Mum, look at that elf, he's moving!"

"Dad, there's a real kitten in the window."

When we went back to Sri Lanka Jan bought over twenty Christmas presents for family, extended family, and children, some of whom she hadn't even met. That's my Jan for you.

Then we went back again for my niece Priyanka, and her husband Joe's twenty-fifth wedding anniversary. It seemed like you couldn't keep us away for too long.

One afternoon late in 2018 my phone rang, I picked up. It was Sharon.

"Hi, Sharon."

"Hi Dad, how have you been?"

"I've been fine, Shazz, you?"

"All good here too. Dad, the reason I'm calling - for a long time I've been wanting to go back to Sri Lanka to see what I had missed out on, the last time I was there. And I was thinking you're not getting any younger, so the sooner I ask you, the better. Will you take me back, please?"

"I'd love to Sharon. Let's make a plan. Leave it with me. I'll call my travel agent, check flights and fares, and check on the availability of Anton, our tour driver in Sri Lanka, the Jetwing travel people in Colombo, and get back to you."

"Thanks, Dad, That'll be awesome."

And so in June of 2019, Sharon and I went back, so she could experience for herself the land of my birth, its culture, and beauty. And all the places she missed out on seeing on that fateful tour twenty-five years before. It was like a pilgrimage for us, to go back together and pick up the threads so tragically cut short all those years ago.

The experience meant a lot to us both and I took her to all my old haunts, - all the places I had told her and Rachel about in bedtime stories of when I was a little boy.

We climbed Sigiriya again. It was a challenge for me this time, but I persevered. The temperature was in the thirties (eighties Fahrenheit). It was humid, and I could feel the sweat trickling down my back as I climbed. I had to stop frequently, and I recalled the times I used to scamper up this very climb in my youth. We reached the Lions Paw staircase at the entrance to the steep steps of the final ascent. I didn't know if Sharon wanted to scale the last challenge to the summit. She did. I did too.

Stopping to catch my breath, I reached my hand out to Sharon for the water bottle from which she was gulping thirstily, water spilling down her neck.

"Here you are," she said, panting. "This is hard work."

"You sure you want to continue to the top? It's pretty steep."

"I'm not going to stop now, after getting this far."

"Well, neither am I."

So we pushed ourselves, encouraged by Anton who kept saying, "You can do this."

"It's only a little bit more."

Now came the final ascent, the steepest set of metal steps on the rock face. But now there were handrails and we pulled ourselves up, up, up slow but steady. We finally reached the summit, and I was happy to have been able to have done it with Sharon. It meant a lot to me. The panoramic view all around made it all worthwhile.

We rested at the top. "Wow. The view is spectacular!" "Isn't it just?" It was just another climb for Anton who did this regularly with his tour groups.

When we were in Kandy, we were driving past the house I lived in when I was four years old. The house from which Dad left to join the Army seventy-six years before. Memories came flooding back to that day, and the very spot from which he got on board that rickshaw to head for the station to leave for Colombo, and out of our lives, for forty-six years.

I asked Anton to pull over so I could get a few pictures. He said, "Why don't you ring the bell and tell whoever is there that you once lived here and would like to take a look around?"

So I did.

A guy answered the door and I said, "Hi! This may come as a surprise, but I once lived here, when I was just four years old." He looked hard at me, deep into my eyes, and with a slight frown on his face said, "What's your name?"

"Robert," I replied. He looked hard at me again.

"You don't know me? I'm Fahmi."

"Fahmi," I said, "Oh! My God! I didn't recognise you after all these years."

We hugged, both overcome with emotion. We had been schoolmates in our teens and had last seen each other sixty-two years before. They had moved into that house when we moved to another and were still there after all these years. The house looked the same and had been well maintained. His brother Iqbal joined us to complete the re-union which was an amazing experience.

We looked around the house and walked out to the back yard from where we watched that train full of soldiers leave for Colombo seventy-six years before.

We spent some time catching up on all the news.

That re-union was the highlight of my visit to Sri Lanka with Sharon.

I have a picture of myself as a four- year- old in 1942 sitting on my Dad's shoulder in a spot in front of the house. At the very same spot I had a picture taken of Sharon and me in 2019 (seventy-seven years later), but she wasn't sitting on my shoulder.

We visited the Botanical Gardens in Kandy, an old haunt of mine, and my niece Susan and her family up in the hills of Bandarawela, before traveling down to the Yala Wildlife Sanctuary. Then a quick visit to my sister and her family, my niece Priyanka and her husband Joe and their two sons Anslem and Jason, and then it was time to head home again to Melbourne.

We'd come full cycle. It was memorable and emotional.

Breaking News!

My grand-daughter Shanti's daughter, Loulani, was born on 17th November 2019. My first great granddaughter.

And now as I potter around in the garden back home in Melbourne, fertilizing roses, pulling out weeds, planting seedlings, or pruning bushes, I often go back in my mind to those days when my passion for gardening was born.

I see, in my mind's eye, as if I were still there, my Uncle Ric, doing the same in his terraced lawn, pushing his manual lawn mower, the smell of freshly mown grass heavy in the air, sweat running down his face, as the twisted blades of the Briggs and Stratton do their work.

And then I'm off in another reverie, thinking how lucky we were to grow up in a town where you could walk out your front door, stroll down the street, take a side road and keep walking, until you find yourself veering off onto a track that leads you through a tea plantation, to a climb that ends up at the top of a mountain.

So many places we explored were within walking distance or a short bus ride away. A walk around Kandy Lake was fifteen minutes away by bus. The fruit orchards we raided were just up the street. It was safe to venture out between dawn and dusk.

Everyone knew everybody else and we all felt we belonged there.

Times were so different then and things have changed. Kandy had a population of 55,000 then. Today that figure is 125,000. The two-lane road outside the house we lived in, which was part of the main road between Colombo and Kandy, is now one part of a thronging divided Highway. Towns, once quiet, leisurely, and peaceful, have turned into bustling, busy boisterous cities.

Once you could walk lazily to school, taking your time, chatting away to schoolmates, with your books slung over your shoulder, laughing and joking as you did. Now that same street is packed with cars, buses, and trucks, bumper to bumper, honking horns, belching out toxic fumes, as drivers swear in frustration.

Yes, times have changed.

It was a different world then when time gave you the full value of its measure and you never felt you had to rush, - unless you were running late for school!

We have so much to be thankful for and I will always be grateful that we grew up in Kandy – Sri Lanka, which was where the foundation was laid for who I am today.

Sigiriya

Early in 2020, I had a dream. I was up in the clouds somewhere. I noticed there was a gap in them and Rachel came through this gap towards me saying, "I've come to get you."

"Can you give me a couple of days? I have some things I need to attend to."

"You'll have to let me know. You know that a day up here is ten years down there."

"Is it because you can only come out just one more time?" She seemed to nod as she turned towards the opening in the clouds. Then she left.

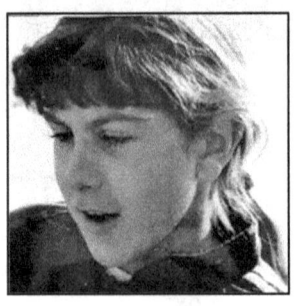

Till we meet again

Author's note

The events in this book are my recollections and not
intended to be a historical record. This is how I
remember them, and this is . . . My Story.

*****

CPSIA information can be obtained
at www.ICGtesting.com
Printed in the USA
BVHW070948040920
588121BV00001B/25

9 781647 187217